120 Bible Stories Activity Book

I0806846

Copyright © 2013 Concordia Publishing House
3558 S. Jefferson Ave., St. Louis, MO 63118-3968
1-800-325-3040 • www.cph.org

All rights reserved. No part of this publication may be reproduced, stored in a retrieval system, or transmitted, in any form or by any means, electronic, mechanical, photocopying, recording, or otherwise, without the prior written permission of Concordia Publishing House.

Prepared by Emily Barz and Alicia Wosepka

Edited by Rodney L. Rathmann

Scripture quotations are from the ESV Bible® (The Holy Bible, English Standard Version®), copyright © 2001 by Crossway Bibles, a publishing ministry of Good News Publishers. Used by permission. All rights reserved.

This publication may be available in Braille, in large print, or on cassette tape for the visually impaired. Please allow 8 to 12 weeks for delivery. Write to Lutheran Braille Workers, P.O. Box 5000, Yucaipa, CA 92399; call toll-free 1-800-925-6092; or visit the Web site: www.LBWinc.org.

Manufactured in the United States of America

4 5 6 7 8 9 10 26 25 24 23

Contents

The Old Testament

The Beginning (Creation to the Flood)

1. God Creates the World (Genesis 1–2) 6
2. The Fall into Sin (Genesis 2–3).................... 7
3. The Children of Adam and Eve (Genesis 4) 8
4. Noah and the Flood (Genesis 6–9) 9

The Patriarchs (2091–1859 BC)

5. God Calls Abram (Genesis 12–13) 10
6. Abram Rescues Lot (Genesis 13–14) 11
7. God's Covenant with Abram (Genesis 15; 17).................... 12
8. Abraham's Visitors (Genesis 18; 21) 13
9. Abraham and Isaac (Genesis 22) 14
10. Isaac and Rebekah (Genesis 24) 15
11. Jacob and Esau (Genesis 25; 27) 16
12. Jacob's Dream (Genesis 27–28) 17
13. Jacob's Family (Genesis 29–31) 18
14. Esau Forgives Jacob (Genesis 32–33).................... 19
15. Joseph's Dreams (Genesis 37).................... 20
16. Joseph in Egypt (Genesis 39–41) 21
17. Joseph Forgives His Brothers (Genesis 42–45) 22
18. Jacob's Blessing (Genesis 45–49).................... 23

Moses and the Return to Canaan (1526–1406 BC)

19. The Birth of Moses (Exodus 1–2) 24
20. God Calls Moses (Exodus 2–4) 25
21. Moses and the Plagues (Exodus 5–10).................... 26
22. The Passover (Exodus 11–13) 27
23. Crossing the Red Sea (Exodus 14–15).................... 28
24. God Provides Manna and Quail (Exodus 16) 29
25. God Gives the Law (Exodus 19–20).................... 30
26. God's Covenant with the Israelites (Exodus 32–34; 40).................... 31
27. The Twelve Spies (Numbers 13–14).................... 32
28. Water from a Rock and Fiery Serpents (Numbers 20–21) 33
29. The Death of Moses (Deuteronomy 18; 31; 34) 34
30. Rahab Hides the Spies (Joshua 1–2) 35
31. Israel Enters the Promised Land (Joshua 3–5) 36
32. The Fall of Jericho (Joshua 6; 24) 37

Judges Rule God's People (1217–1060 BC)

33. Deborah the Prophetess (Judges 2; 4–5) 38
34. Gideon Defeats Midian (Judges 6–8) 39
35. God Makes Samson Strong (Judges 13; 15–16) 40
36. Ruth (The Book of Ruth) 41
37. Hannah and Samuel (1 Samuel 1–2) 42
38. God Calls Samuel (1 Samuel 2–4) 43

Great Prophets and Kings (1049–587 BC)

39. Saul Becomes King (1 Samuel 8–11) 44
40. Samuel Anoints David (1 Samuel 15–16) 45
41. David Fights Goliath (1 Samuel 17) 46
42. David and Jonathan (1 Samuel 18; 20) 47
43. God's Covenant with David (2 Samuel 7) 48
44. Solomon Becomes King (1 Kings 2–3) 49
45. Solomon Builds the Temple (1 Kings 5–6; 8) 50
46. God Provides for Elijah (1 Kings 16–17) 51
47. Elijah and the Prophets of Baal (1 Kings 18) 52
48. God Takes Elijah to Heaven (1 Kings 19; 2 Kings 2) 53
49. Naaman and Elisha (2 Kings 5) 54
50. Jonah (The Book of Jonah) 55
51. Isaiah Sees the Lord (Isaiah 6–7; 9; 53) 56
52. King Hezekiah Prays (2 Kings 18–19) 57
53. King Josiah (2 Kings 22–23) 58
54. God Calls Jeremiah (Jeremiah 1; 23; 31) 59

God's People in Exile (722–533 BC)

55. Israel and Judah in Exile (2 Kings 17; 24–25) 60
56. God's Promises to the Exiles (Ezekiel 8; 36) 61
57. Three Men in the Fiery Furnace (Daniel 3) 62
58. Daniel in the Lions' Den (Daniel 6) 63
59. Daniel Sees Heaven (Daniel 7) 64

God's People Return to Judah (538–430 BC)

60. A New Temple and a New Wall (The Books of Ezra; Nehemiah) 65
61. Esther and the King (Esther 1–2) 66
62. God Saves His People (Esther 3–8) 67
63. Waiting for God's Messenger (The Book of Malachi) 68

The New Testament

Jesus' Childhood (4 BC–AD 11)

64. The Birth of John Foretold (Luke 1) 69
65. The Birth of Jesus Foretold (Luke 1; Matthew 1) 70
66. The Birth of John (Luke 1) 71
67. The Birth of Jesus (Luke 2) 72
68. The Visit of the Wise Men (Matthew 2) 73
69. The Boy Jesus in the Temple (Luke 2) 74

Jesus' Public Ministry (AD 29–32)

70. John Baptizes Jesus (Matthew 3; John 1) 75
71. The Temptation of Jesus (Matthew 4) 76
72. Jesus Calls Disciples (John 1; Luke 5) 77
73. Jesus Changes Water into Wine (John 2) 78
74. Jesus Clears the Temple (John 2) 79
75. Jesus Teaches Nicodemus (John 3) 80

76. Jesus and the Samaritan Woman (John 4) 81
77. Jesus Rejected at Nazareth (Luke 4) 82
78. Jesus Heals a Paralyzed Man (Mark 2) 83
79. The Sermon on the Mount (Matthew 5–7) 84
80. Jesus Calms a Storm (Mark 4) 85
81. Jesus Heals Jairus's Daughter (Mark 5) 86
82. Jesus Feeds Five Thousand (John 6) 87
83. Jesus Walks on Water (Matthew 14) 88
84. Jesus Is Anointed (Luke 7) 89
85. Peter's Confession and Jesus' Transfiguration (Matthew 16; Mark 9) 90
86. Jesus Sends the Seventy-Two (Luke 10) 91
87. The Good Samaritan (Luke 10) 92
88. Jesus Heals a Blind Man (John 9) 93
89. The Good Shepherd (John 10; Psalm 23) 94
90. Jesus Raises Lazarus (John 11) 95
91. The Prodigal Son (Luke 15) 96
92. Jesus Heals Ten Men (Luke 17) 97
93. Jesus and the Little Children (Mark 9–10) 98
94. Jesus and Zacchaeus (Luke 19) 99

Jesus' Passion, Death, and Resurrection (AD 33)

95. The Triumphal Entry (Matthew 21; Mark 11; Luke 19) 100
96. The Widow's Coins (Mark 12) 101
97. The Lord's Supper (Luke 22) 102
98. Jesus in the Garden (Matthew 26; Mark 14; Luke 22) 103
99. Peter Denies Jesus (Matthew 26) 104
100. Jesus' Trial (Matthew 27; John 18) 105
101. The Crucifixion (Matthew 17; Luke 23; John 19) 106
102. The Resurrection (Luke 24; John 20) 107
103. Jesus Appears on the Emmaus Road (Luke 24) 108
104. Jesus Appears to Thomas (John 20) 109
105. Jesus and Peter (John 21) 110
106. Jesus Ascends to Heaven (Matthew 28; Acts 1) 111

The Holy Spirit Leads God's Church (AD 33–95)

107. Pentecost (Acts 2) 112
108. Peter and John Heal a Lame Man (Acts 3) 113
109. God's Servant Stephen (Acts 6–7) 114
110. Philip and the Ethiopian (Acts 8) 115
111. The Conversion of Saul (Acts 9) 116
112. Peter and Cornelius (Acts 10) 117
113. Peter's Escape from Prison (Acts 12) 118
114. Paul's First Missionary Journey (Acts 13–14) 119
115. Paul and Timothy (Acts 16; the Books of 1 and 2 Timothy) 120
116. Paul Tells Lydia about Christ (Acts 16)/
Paul Writes to Philippians (Philippians 1; 4) 121
117. Paul and Silas in Prison (Acts 16) 122
118. Paul's Letters (The Books of Romans; Ephesians; 1 Thessalonians) 123
119. Paul Sails to Rome (Acts 27–28) 124
120. John's Vision of Heaven (Revelation 21–22) 125

1

God Creates the World (Genesis 1–2)

Reviewing God's Word

The first two chapters of Genesis describe the plan God followed for each day of creation. The first three days are sometimes referred to as days of forming, and the next three days are sometimes called days of filling. On the days of forming, God called into being. On the days of filling, God built upon the work of the days of forming.

Draw a line to match each day of forming with its corresponding day of filling:

Day 1: Light and darkness	Day 5: Sea creatures and birds
Day 2: Sky and water	Day 6: Animals and people
Day 3: Dry ground and vegetation	Day 4: Sun, moon, and stars

Thinking about God's Word

1. What is meant by "the beginning"?

2. Who lived before the beginning?

3. Out of what did God make the world?

4. In John 1:1–3, Jesus, the Son of God, is called "the Word." What connection is there between "the Word" and "God said"?

5. What were the chief differences between people and the other moving creatures?

6. Who is meant by "Us" and "Our" when God speaks about making people?

7. Which words tell that there was not a mistake or a flaw in anything God had made?

8. What did God create on the seventh day?

9. All Scripture points to God and His love for us in Christ Jesus. How does God's designation of the seventh day remind us of Jesus? See Matthew 11:28.

Applying God's Word

1. In what way does God continue to create the world today?

2. What does God's Word accomplish in our lives today?

3. How do the teachings of evolution compare with those of Genesis 1?

2

The Fall into Sin
(Genesis 2–3)

Reviewing God's Word

Underline the word or phrase that answers each question.

1. Whose fault was it that Adam sinned?
   (Devil's—Adam's—God's—Eve's)
2. Whose fault was it that Eve sinned?
   (Devil's—Serpent's—God's—Eve's)
3. Who drove Adam and his wife from the garden?
   (Devil—Cherubim—God—Wild animals)
4. Why did Adam and his wife try to hide from God?
   (They were naked—They were like God—
   They had sinned—They didn't know God)
5. How did God punish Adam, his wife, and the serpent?
   (He cursed them—He killed them—
   He abandoned them—He hid from them)
6. Who are sinners? (Only heathens—All people
   Everyone except Christians—Only adults)
7. For whose sake did God curse the ground? (God's sake—
   The woman's sake—Adam's sake—Satan's sake)

Thinking about God's Word

1. How did God communicate with Adam and Eve?

2. What special command had God given them?

3. How did the first two people become disobedient?

4. Why did Adam and Eve hide from God?

5. How did Adam and Eve try to make excuses for their sin?

6. Name four evils that have come into the world because of sin.

7. What sentence did God pronounce on the woman?

   on the man?

Applying God's Word

1. What tactic did the devil successfully use to tempt Adam and Eve to sin?

   Does the devil ever use this temptation with you?

2. Why did Adam and Eve's relationship with God change when they sinned?

   How does sin hurt your relationship with God?

3. How did Jesus, the offspring of Eve, crush the head of the serpent?

   How has Jesus' work changed your relationship with God?

3

The Children of Adam and Eve (Genesis 4)

Reviewing God's Word

Fill in the blanks, using the words below. Some words may be used more than once or not at all.

1. __________ was the first child born to Adam and Eve.
2. Adam and Eve's second child was named __________.
3. Cain was a __________________.
4. Abel was a __________________.
5. The offering that ____________ brought pleased God.
6. ________________ committed the first murder.
7. God cursed Cain and made him a ______________.
8. Adam and Eve's third son was named ____________.

Cain	Enosh	Seth	Adam
slave	farmer	shepherd	wanderer
Abel	Nod	fisherman	hunter

Thinking about God's Word

1. Whom did Eve credit for the birth of her son?

2. What is one way Cain and Abel worshiped God?

3. What warning did Cain receive from God?

4. What did Cain ask God in order to try to avoid responsibility for Abel's murder?

5. What curse did God put on Cain?

6. Was the mark that God set on Cain a blessing or a punishment?

   Why?

7. How did God show mercy to Adam and Eve?

Applying God's Word

1. How does God's warning to Cain apply to all people?

2. Answer Cain's question correctly and give a reason for your answer: "Am I my brother's keeper?"

3. God had promised that a Savior would come through Adam's descendants. Then one of Adam's sons was killed and the other was exiled. How did God continue His plan for salvation?

   What does this tell us about God?

4

Noah and the Flood
(Genesis 6–9)

Reviewing God's Word

Answer each question by circling Yes or No.

1. Did God send a flood to destroy the world because the people were wicked?	YES	NO
2. Did the flood cover only part of the earth?	YES	NO
3. Were the mountains covered with water?	YES	NO
4. Did God forget about Noah and his family?	YES	NO
5. Did the ark come to rest on Ararat?	YES	NO
6. Were all people and animals (other than those on the ark) destroyed by the flood?	YES	NO
7. Does God punish wickedness today?	YES	NO

Thinking about God's Word

1. What did the Lord see that made Him grieve?

2. What did the Lord plan to do?

3. How was Noah different from the other people?

4. What did God tell Noah to do?

5. How did Noah show that he believed God?

6. Which people were saved by the ark?

7. What did Noah do after leaving the ark?

8. What promise from God did the rainbow symbolize?

Applying God's Word

1. Why did God declare Noah righteous? See Hebrews 11:7.

   How are we declared righteous?

2. God could probably say the same thing about our world that He said about Noah's: The wickedness of man is great and all man thinks about is doing evil. What comfort can we find in the account of the flood?

3. The great flood reminds us of the Sacrament of Holy Baptism. See 1 Peter 3:18–22. Explain.

5

God Calls Abram
(Genesis 12–13)

Reviewing God's Word

Draw lines to connect each cause to its effect.

Cause:	Effect:
1. God told Abram to go to a land He would show him.	• Lot moved to the Jordan valley.
2. God promised Canaan to Abram's descendants.	• Abram went to Egypt.
3. There was a famine in Canaan.	• God sent a plague on Pharaoh's house.
4. Abram was worried he would be killed.	• Abram built an altar to God.
5. Pharaoh took Sarai into his house.	• Abram said Sarai was his sister.
6. Abram and Lot's herdsmen fought.	• Abram moved to Canaan.

Thinking about God's Word

1. What command came to Abram, whom God later named Abraham, from the Lord?

2. What threefold promise did God give with His command?

3. Which of these promises meant the same as the promise given to Adam and Eve after the fall?

4. How did Abram worship God in public after he arrived in Canaan?

5. Why did Abram lie to Pharaoh about Sarai being his wife?

6. How did Abram keep peace between himself and his nephew?

7. What promise did God make to Abram about his offspring?

Applying God's Word

1. In what way have all people on earth been blessed through Abraham?

2. How did Abram show his faith in God? See Hebrews 11:8.

   How do we show our faith in God?

3. Abram took things into his own hands while in Egypt, rather than trusting God for protection. When do you have the most trouble trusting God? What application for your own life can you find in the fact that God delivered Abram and Sarai?

6

Abram Rescues Lot (Genesis 13–14)

Reviewing God's Word

Fill in the blanks, using the words below.

1. Abram settled in the land of ______________, while Lot settled among the cities of the valley.
2. The kings of Sodom and __________________ were on the losing side.
3. The enemy also took _____________, who was living in Sodom, and his possessions.
4. Melchizedek, the king of Salem, brought out ____________________ and wine.
5. Melchizedek said, "Blessed be Abram by God Most High, _________________ of heaven and earth."
6. Abram said to the king of Sodom, "I would not take a ___________ or a sandal strap or anything that is yours."

Possessor	Canaan	bread
Lot	thread	Gomorrah

Thinking about God's Word

1. What happened in the Jordan Valley, where Lot had chosen to live?

2. What did the winning kings take as plunder?

3. What did Abram do when he heard what had happened?

4. Whom did Abram meet after returning from defeating the enemy kings?

5. What did Abram do when he met this person?

Applying God's Word

1. God used Abram to rescue Lot. How has God used other people to rescue you from bad situations?

2. Melchizedek brought out bread and wine to celebrate God's deliverance. What church celebration does this remind you of?

3. How is Jesus like Melchizedek?

7

God's Covenant with Abram (Genesis 15; 17)

Reviewing God's Word

God often used names very deliberately because of their specific meaning.

Using your knowledge of these people, match each name to its meaning.

1. Abraham	A person of royalty
2. Sarah	The Lord saves
3. Isaac	Father of a multitude
4. Jesus	He laughs

Thinking about God's Word

1. How did God comfort Abram's fears?

2. How did God answer him when Abram said he was still childless?

3. Why did it take great faith for Abram to believe this promise?

4. What did God do as a sign of His covenant with Abram?

5. When did God say Abraham's son would be born?

6. What does it mean to believe in God?

Applying God's Word

1. Abraham believed the Lord, and He credited it to him as righteousness. How is God's righteousness credited to people today?

2. Abraham asked for one child, and God promised that his descendants would be as numerous as the stars. In what ways has God given you even more than you could ask for or think of? See Ephesians 3:20.

3. In addition to Abraham's actual descendants, who else is included among the children of Abraham? See Galatians 3:29.

8

Abraham's Visitors (Genesis 18; 21)

Reviewing God's Word

Underline the word or phrase that answers each question.

1. Who were the three men who came to Abraham's tent? (The Lord and two angels—Pharaoh and two servants—the King of Sodom and two officials—Melchizedek and two priests)
2. What did Abraham offer to his guests? (A place to sleep—Money—Water and a meal—A donkey to ride)
3. What did Abraham tell Sarah to do? (Bring water—Bake cakes—Prepare a calf—Clean the tent)
4. How old was Abraham when Isaac was born? (99—90—95—100)
5. How did Sarah say people would respond to the news of Isaac's birth? (They would cry—They would laugh—They would sing for joy—They would be speechless)

Thinking about God's Word

1. In what form did the Lord come to Abraham at the time of this story?

2. What special message did the Lord bring to Abraham?

3. How did Abraham show hospitality?

4. How did Sarah hear the Lord's promise, even though it was not spoken directly to her?

5. How would you answer the question "Why did Sarah laugh?"

6. Why did it make sense for the child to be named Isaac (meaning "he laughs")?

Applying God's Word

1. What characteristic of God is suggested by the question "Is anything too hard for God?"

2. Name a promise God has made to us that has not yet been fulfilled. Do you believe it will be fulfilled? Why can we trust God to keep all of His promises?

3. In this account, God took on human form to visit His people. When else did God take on human form to live among His people? See Galatians 4:4–5.

9

Abraham and Isaac (Genesis 22)

Reviewing God's Word

Fill in the blanks, using the words below.

1. God ____________________ Abraham.
2. God told Abraham, "Take your only son, Isaac, whom you love, and go to the land of Moriah. Offer him there as a bu rnt ____________________."
3. Abraham said, "I and the boy will go over there and ____________________ and come again to you."
4. "God will ____________________ for Himself the lamb for a burnt offering."
5. Then Abraham took the knife to ____________________ his son.
6. The Lord said, "Now I know that you ____________________ God, seeing you have not withheld your only son from Me."
7. "In your offspring shall all the nations of the earth be ____________________, because you have obeyed My voice."

kill	provide	tested	worship
offering	fear	blessed	

Thinking about God's Word

1. How did God test Abraham?

2. Why must God's command have been a shock to Abraham?

3. Yet, what did Abraham's faith in God move him to do in answer to God's command?

4. In which words did the angel of the Lord tell Abraham that he had passed the test?

5. What did the angel of the Lord say Abraham's blessing would be?

6. Name three ways in which Abraham's son and God's Son were the same.

7. God spared Abraham's son, but what did He do with His own Son?

Applying God's Word

1. What things do you love most? Would you be willing to sacrifice them or give them up to God? What great sacrifice did God make for us?

2. What was Abraham's answer to Isaac's question?

   With what action did God fulfill a short time later what Abraham said and believed?

   What Lamb did God Himself provide as an offering about 2,000 years later?

3. What did Abraham believe God would do to restore Isaac if he would have sacrificed his son? See Hebrews 11:17–19. Of what great event does this belief remind us?

10

Isaac and Rebekah
(Genesis 24)

Reviewing God's Word

Draw a line through the sentences that are not true.

1. Abraham sent his servant to get a wife for Isaac.
2. The servant searched the whole city of Nahor for the right woman.
3. The servant chose Rebekah because she was the prettiest woman he saw.
4. Rebekah's father was Bethuel.
5. Laban welcomed the servant into his home.
6. Laban and Bethuel agreed that Rebekah should go with the servant.
7. Rebekah had fallen in love with Isaac.
8. Isaac and Rebekah married, and Isaac loved his wife.

Thinking about God's Word

1. Why did Abraham send his servant back to his homeland?

2. What did the servant do when he arrived in Nahor?

3. How did the servant know that Rebekah was the chosen woman?

   What does this say about Rebekah?

4. What did Laban do when he heard about the servant?

5. Why did Laban and Bethuel agree to send Rebekah with the servant?

6. How did Rebekah show her faith in God?

Applying God's Word

1. Why was it important for the servant to go to Abraham's homeland to find a wife for Isaac?

2. What did the servant do before—and after— finding Rebekah?

   How can you follow his example?

3. Abraham, the servant, Laban, Bethuel, Rebekah, and Isaac all trusted that God had a plan for this marriage. Why was Isaac's marriage to Rebekah so important for God's great plan of salvation?

11

Jacob and Esau (Genesis 25; 27)

Reviewing God's Word

Answer each question with either *Esau* or *Jacob*.

1. Who was the older son?
2. To whom did Isaac wish to give the blessing?
3. Whom did Rebekah want to get the blessing?
4. When Jacob came in to see his father, who did he say he was?
5. Whom did Isaac think he heard speaking when Jacob was in the room?
5. Whom did Isaac think Jacob was when he felt Jacob's hands?
6. To whom did Isaac give the blessing of the firstborn?

Thinking about God's Word

1. In what way were both Esau and Jacob gifts from God?

2. How does this remind you of Isaac's birth?

3. What did Jacob give Esau in exchange for his birthright?

4. How did Rebekah try to take things into her own hands?

5. What lie did Jacob speak to his father?

6. Why could Jacob fool his father so easily?

7. Why did Jacob flee to Laban?

Applying God's Word

1. How did Jacob break each of the following commandments?

   IV. Honor your father and your mother.

   VII. You shall not steal.

2. Of what was Rebekah guilty?

3. What do Jesus' life, death, and resurrection mean for all repentant sinners?

12

Jacob's Dream
(Genesis 27–28)

Reviewing God's Word

Write the name of the speaker next to each quote. Names may be used more than once or not at all.

1. "God Almighty bless you and make you fruitful and multiply you."
2. "The land on which you lie I will give to you and to your offspring."
3. "This is the gate of heaven."
4. "Take as your wife one of the daughters of Laban."
5. "This is none other than the house of God."
6. "Behold, I am with you and will keep you wherever you go."

God	Jacob	Isaac
Rebekah	Esau	Laban

Thinking about God's Word

1. Why did Isaac send Jacob to the house of Laban?

2. How did God appear to Jacob?

3. What vision did Jacob see in his dream?

4. What blessing did God give to Jacob?

5. What name did Jacob give to the place where he had his dream?

6. What vow did Jacob make before he left Bethel?

7. Have you ever been blessed by someone? When? Where? How? Why?

Applying God's Word

1. Jacob received the blessing God gave to Abraham. What was the most significant part of that blessing?

2. In what ways do God's angels serve His people?

3. How is Bethel like a Christian church?

13

Jacob's Family
(Genesis 29–31)

Reviewing God's Word

Fill in the blanks, using the words below. Some words will not be used.

1. Jacob traveled to the land of the people of the _________.
2. Rachel was Laban's ____________________________.
3. Jacob agreed to work _______________ years for Rachel.
4. Laban gave Jacob _______________ in marriage instead.
5. Jacob loved ______________________ more than Leah.
6. God told Jacob to return to ______________________.

Dinah	west	daughter	Nod
Leah	seven	Canaan	Rachel
five	sister	North	east

Thinking about God's Word

1. Why was Jacob so excited to meet Rachel?

2. How many daughters did Laban have?

3. Why did Jacob agree to work for Laban for seven years?

4. How did Laban trick Jacob?

5. How much longer did Jacob work in order to marry Rachel?

6. Which words show that God gave Jacob many gifts while he was working for Laban?

7. What did the Lord tell Jacob to do?

8. Why did Jacob not have to fear the long journey back to Canaan and back to a brother who had threatened to kill him?

Applying God's Word

1. Jacob's earlier trickery and Laban's deceit caused conflict within their families, yet God was at work through it all. What conflicts does your family have, and how might God bring good out of these situations?

2. Jacob was blessed with twelve sons. Twelve is an important number in the Bible to represent the whole people of God. Can you think of another important group of twelve men in the Bible?

3. Jacob knew it would be hard to move his whole family back to Canaan and face his brother, Esau, but he trusted that God would be with him. What hard things can you get through knowing that God is always with you?

14

Esau Forgives Jacob
(Genesis 32–33)

Reviewing God's Word

Underline the word or phrase that makes each sentence true.

1. In his message to Esau, Jacob called himself Esau's (slave—master—servant—hired hand).
2. Jacob told God he wasn't worthy of His (wrath—punishment—steadfast love—anger).
3. (God—An angel—Satan—Esau) wrestled with Jacob at night.
4. God changed Jacob's name to (Isaac—Israel—Abraham—Shechem).
5. Esau (hated—punished—exiled—forgave) Jacob.

Thinking about God's Word

1. What did Jacob send his messengers to tell Esau?

2. Why did Jacob think Esau might attack him and his household?

3. How did Jacob show humility in his prayer for protection?

4. What blessing did God give to Jacob after they wrestled?

5. What did Esau do when Jacob came to him and bowed before him?

6. What did Jacob do when he was safely in Canaan with his entire household?

Applying God's Word

1. Jacob remembered in his prayer that he was unworthy of God's love and faithfulness, yet he still prayed for deliverance. Why can we pray for God's blessings, even though we don't deserve them?

2. God changed Jacob's name from Jacob (meaning "he cheats") to Israel (meaning "he who wrestles with God and wins"). How was God setting the stage for more change in Jacob's life?

3. In the Lord's Prayer, we pray that God would "forgive us our trespasses as we forgive those who trespass against us." What prompts you, like Esau, to show forgiveness to others?

15

Joseph's Dreams
(Genesis 37)

Reviewing God's Word

Draw lines to match each person to his action(s).

1. Israel/Jacob	• Showed favoritism
	• Sold Joseph to the Ishmaelites
2. Joseph	• Dreamed about sheaves and the sun, moon, and stars
	• Remembered Joseph's dreams
3. Reuben	• Threw Joseph in a pit
	• Tried to rescue Joseph
	• Mourned without being comforted
4. The brothers	• Dipped Joseph's robe in blood

Thinking about God's Word

1. Why did Joseph's brothers hate him?

2. How did Jacob show his great love for Joseph?

3. What did Joseph's dreams mean?

4. Why did Israel send Joseph to find his brothers?

5. How did the brothers show their hatred for Joseph and their hard-heartedness?

6. How did the brothers deceive their father?

7. How did the brothers hurt Joseph, Jacob, and most of all, themselves?

Applying God's Word

1. How is Jacob as a father like our Father in heaven? How is he different?

2. Jacob gave Joseph a beautiful robe to wear. With what are those who have been baptized into Christ clothed? See Galatians 3:27 and Revelation 7:13–14.

3. Reuben pleaded with his brothers for Joseph's life, but in the end, he couldn't rescue him. Who pleads with God on our behalf and did rescue us?

16

Joseph in Egypt
(Genesis 39–41)

Reviewing God's Word

Underline the word or phrase that best completes each sentence.

1. Joseph (exposed—gave in to—fled—enjoyed) the temptations of Potiphar's wife.
2. But Potiphar (jailed—praised—promoted—exiled) Joseph.
3. The cupbearer told Pharaoh about Joseph (immediately—2 weeks later—2 years later—never).
4. Pharaoh was the (king—captain—president—prince) of Egypt.
5. Joseph said that (he—magicians—Jacob—God) would answer Pharaoh.
6. Pharaoh's dreams told about (14—7—10—8) years of famine.
7. The famine was severe all over (Egypt—Canaan—Ur—the earth).

Thinking about God's Word

1. How did Joseph show that he wanted to do the right thing and follow God's commands?
2. How did God bless Joseph even while he was in prison?
3. What did Joseph do for the cupbearer and baker while they were in prison?
4. Why did Pharaoh have to find someone in place of his magicians to interpret his dreams?
5. How did Pharaoh know that Joseph could interpret dreams?
6. How did Joseph show his humility as he stood before Pharaoh?
7. What advice did Joseph give Pharaoh together with the interpretation?
8. Whom did Pharaoh put in charge?

Applying God's Word

1. How did God show Joseph His steadfast love even when things weren't going well?
2. What words of Joseph show that the power to interpret dreams wasn't his own?
3. God was faithful to Joseph and gave him a position of prominence in Egypt, but he was in prison for two years first. What does this say about God's timing?

17

Joseph Forgives His Brothers (Genesis 42–45)

Reviewing God's Word

Circle Yes or No for each statement.

1. Jacob went with Joseph's brothers to Egypt to get grain.	YES	NO
2. Joseph's brothers recognized him.	YES	NO
3. Joseph kept Simeon bound in Egypt.	YES	NO
4. Joseph invited his brothers to eat with him.	YES	NO
5. Reuben received the most food.	YES	NO
6. Benjamin stole Joseph's silver cup.	YES	NO
7. Judah offered to stay as a slave instead of Benjamin.	YES	NO
8. Joseph punished his brothers for how they mistreated him.	YES	NO

Thinking about God's Word

1. How can you tell that there was a famine also in Canaan during the lean years?

2. What did Joseph do to his brothers when they came to him?

3. Why might the brothers have not recognized Joseph?

4. How did the brothers react when they reached home and found their money in their sacks?

5. Whom did Jacob send with the brothers the second time they went to Egypt?

6. Why did Joseph put the cup was in Benjamin's sack?

7. How did the words of Judah show that his heart was changed?

8. How can you tell that this is what Joseph had hoped for in testing his brothers?

Applying God's Word

1. How could Joseph easily have taken revenge on his brothers for having sold him?

   Why didn't he?

2. Judah was willing to give himself up for his brother Benjamin. What prominent New Testament figure was born from Judah's descendants (Matthew 1:1–16)? Why is this significant?

3. Although we have sinned against God worse than Joseph's brothers sinned against him, why can we come to God without fear?

18

Jacob's Blessing
(Genesis 45–49)

Reviewing God's Word

Write the name of the speaker next to each quote.

1. "Say to your brothers, 'Come to me. I will give you the best of the land of Egypt.'"
2. "Now let me die, since I have seen your face and know that you are still alive."
3. "Joseph is ruler over all Egypt."
4. "The scepter shall not depart from Judah, nor the ruler's staff from between his feet."
5. "Do not be afraid to go to Egypt. There I will make you into a great nation."
6. "Do not bury me in Egypt, but let me lie with my fathers."

God	Joseph	The brothers
Israel/Jacob	Pharaoh	Judah

Thinking about God's Word

1. Why did Joseph send wagons to Canaan?
2. What did Pharaoh promise to Joseph's family?
3. What did Israel do before he went to Egypt?
4. How did Jacob and Joseph show how overjoyed they were to be reunited?
5. Whom did Jacob bless first?
6. What was the special blessing Jacob gave to Judah?
7. Why does this blessing make sense in light of Judah's descendants?
8. Where did Jacob ask to be buried?

Applying God's Word

1. How did Joseph show his love for his family?

   What are some specific ways you can show love to your family?

2. Read Romans 8:28. What things seemed evil in Joseph's life?

   How did God work for good in all things?

3. Although Ephraim and Manasseh were born in Egypt to an Egyptian mother, they were blessed by Jacob and adopted in as full children of Israel. How has God adopted you?

19

The Birth of Moses
(Exodus 1–2)

Reviewing God's Word

Fill in the blanks.

1. The more the people of Israel were ________________, the more they multiplied.
2. The king of Egypt told the midwives, "When you serve as midwife to the Hebrew women, if it is a son, you shall ________________ him."
3. When Moses' mother could hide him no longer, she made a ________________________ of bulrushes.
4. Moses' ________________ stood at a distance to know what would be done to him.
5. Pharaoh's daughter took ____________ on baby Moses and said, "This is one of the Hebrews' children."
6. Pharaoh's daughter asked Moses' mother to __________ baby Moses for her.
7. When Moses had grown up, he saw an _____________ beating a Hebrew, one of his people.
8. But Moses fled from Pharaoh and stayed in the land of ______________________.

Thinking about God's Word

1. How did the Lord bless the family of Israel in Egypt?

   Why didn't the new pharaoh like this?

2. How did Pharaoh try to stop the growth of the Israelites?

3. How do you explain the fact that "the more they were oppressed, the more they multiplied"?

   Of which blessing of God to Abraham does this remind you?

4. Think of two good reasons why the Levite woman did not drown her son.

   Why did she not keep him at home longer?

5. How were the mother and daughter wise in placing Moses in the rushes?

   What did God have to do with their wisdom?

6. Why did the princess keep the baby she found?

7. Who gave Moses his name?

   Why did she name him Moses?

8. What evidence does this story provide to indicate that Moses identified himself with the people of God rather than with the Egyptians?

Applying God's Word

1. How does this account show that God is more powerful than human rulers?

2. Why might it have been hard for Moses to identify with the people of God?

   Is it ever easier for you to identify with other people who seem to have it all rather than with God's people?

3. Compare the birth of Jesus and the birth of Moses.

20

God Calls Moses
(Exodus 2–4)

Reviewing God's Word

Underline the word or phrase that answers each question.

1. What did the people of Israel do because of their slavery?
   (Sulked—Cried out for help—Refused to work—Turned their backs on God)
2. What did God tell Moses to do in His presence?
   (Fall to the ground—Perform ceremonial washing—Take off his sandals—Be silent)
3. What else did Moses do to show that he feared God?
   (Hid his face—Ran away—Trembled with fear—Refused to speak)
4. What did God promise would be in the Promised Land?
   (Green pastures—Flowing water—Rich farmland—Milk and honey)
5. What did the people do when Aaron spoke to them?
   (Wept—Laughed—Believed and worshiped—Rebelled against Egypt)

Thinking about God's Word

1. Why did God appear to Moses?

2. How did the Lord appear to Moses?

3. Why did the Lord call the Hebrews "My people"?

   Why did the Lord want to help His people?

4. What name for Himself did God give Moses to tell to the people?

5. What signs did God give Moses?

6. What was Moses' excuse for why he couldn't go?

7. What did God promise in response to Moses' excuse?

8. How did the Lord patiently answer Moses when he pleaded with Him to send someone else?

Applying God's Word

1. Why was Moses hesitant to go to Pharaoh to free the Israelites?

   Do you ever feel unqualified to do what God has called you to do?

   What comfort can you find in God's dealings with Moses?

2. God told Moses to tell the people that "I AM" had sent him. Who else used the phrase "I am" to describe Himself? See John 8:58, as well as numerous other passages in John's Gospel.

   Why is this important?

3. Who are the leaders of God's people today?

   How are they like Moses?

21

Moses and the Plagues (Exodus 5–10)

Reviewing God's Word

God used the plagues to show the Egyptians that He alone was God. Many of the plagues even corresponded to specific Egyptian gods or values that the real God displayed His power over.

Draw lines to match these plagues to the Egyptian god or value they were directed against.

1. Nile turned to blood	• Flies and beetles honored in worship
2. Frogs	• Herds and flocks symbolized wealth
3. Flies	• Hapi (Nile god and giver of life)
4. Death of livestock	• Crops meant food and income
5. Boils	• Ra (Egyptian sun god)
6. Hail	• Personal health and strength
7. Darkness	• Heqt (Frog goddess of childbirth)

Thinking about God's Word

1. How did Moses and Aaron let Pharaoh know that they were sent by God?

2. How did Pharaoh respond?

3. How did the magicians do some of the signs Moses did?

4. Why did God say He would harden Pharaoh's heart and bring plagues on Egypt?

5. Whom did the later plagues affect?

6. How did Pharaoh respond to the plague of darkness?

Applying God's Word

1. God sent the miraculous plagues to prove to the Egyptians that He was God. How is this like Jesus' miracles? See John 20:30–31.

2. God struck down all of the Egyptians' sources of life: water from the Nile, food from livestock, and even light from the sun. What was He proving?

   How does God move us to respond to His blessings?

3. In the ninth plague, God sent darkness over all of Egypt. What do darkness and light often represent in the Bible? See John 8:12.

22

The Passover (Exodus 11–13)

Reviewing God's Word

Draw a line through the statements that were NOT part of God's instructions for the Passover.

1. Take a lamb for each household.
2. Each lamb should be two years old.
3. The Passover lamb must be a female.
4. Kill the lamb at twilight.
5. Spread blood on the doorposts and lintels.
6. Eat the lamb with unleavened bread and bitter herbs.
7. Save some of the meat for the journey.
8. Savor every bite of the special meal.
9. Eat with your belt fastened and sandals on your feet.

Thinking about God's Word

1. What was the last plague God sent?

2. What would keep death from coming over the firstborn of the children of Israel?

3. What did God want to show by this plague?

4. How was the final plague a devastating blow to the Egyptians?

5. How were the Israelites supposed to celebrate the Passover festival in the future?

6. Why were the Israelites supposed to celebrate the Passover every year?

7. How did God lead His people out of Egypt?

Applying God's Word

1. Who is our Passover lamb?

   How did He become a Passover lamb for us? See 1 Corinthians 5:7.

2. What celebratory meal did Jesus institute while He was sharing the Passover with His disciples? See Luke 22:7–20.

3. How did the children of Israel show that they believed the Lord?

   How do we show that we believe in God? See 1 John 5:3–4.

23

Crossing the Red Sea (Exodus 14–15)

Reviewing God's Word

Write the name of the speaker next to each quote.

1. "What is this we have done, that we have let Israel go from serving us?"
2. "Fear not. Stand firm. See the salvation of the LORD."
3. "Stretch out your hand over the sea, that the water may come back."
4. "What have you done to us in bringing us out of Egypt?"
5. "Let us flee from before Israel, for the LORD fights for them."
6. "I will sing to the LORD, for He has triumphed gloriously."

God	Moses	Egyptians
Israelites	Pharaoh	Moses/Israel

Thinking about God's Word

1. Why did Pharaoh want the Israelites back?
2. What did Moses say to reassure the people when they saw the Egyptians chasing them?
3. What miracle did God perform through Moses to enable the people to cross the Red Sea?
4. How did God bring chaos to the Egyptian army?
5. What do you suppose the Egyptians thought when they rushed into the Red Sea after the children of Israel?
6. How did the Lord finally punish proud Pharaoh and his army in which he trusted?
7. How did the Israelites thank God for His wonderful deliverance?

Applying God's Word

1. God came to His people Israel in a pillar of cloud and in a pillar of fire. How does God come to His people today? What visible signs of His presence does He give us?
2. God rescued His people from captivity in Egypt. From what forms of captivity has God rescued us?
3. Moses and the Israelites responded to God's deliverance with a song of praise to God. What are some great things God has done in your life that you can praise Him for?

24

God Provides Manna and Quail
(Exodus 16)

Reviewing God's Word

Draw a line through the sentences that are not true.

1. The Israelites were so hungry that they wished they had died in Egypt.
2. Moses provided food for the people.
3. God ignored the people because they were complaining too much.
4. God provided manna to show the Israelites that He was the Lord.
5. The Israelites were not supposed to have any manna left over each day.
6. All the people followed God's instructions.
7. God gave special instructions for the seventh day.
8. God provided manna for the people every day until they reached the Promised Land.

Thinking about God's Word

1. Why did the Israelites grumble?

2. How did the Lord promise to feed them?

   How did He keep His promise?

3. What instructions did God give the people about the manna?

4. Why was Moses angry with the Israelites?

5. What were God's special instructions about the Sabbath Day?

Applying God's Word

1. God gave His people Israel special food from heaven. What special meal has God given us?

2. Why do you think God let the people collect only enough manna for one day? What could we learn from this?

3. God commanded the Israelites to rest on the Sabbath and not collect manna that day. How do we honor the Sabbath today?

25

God Gives the Law
(Exodus 19–20)

Reviewing God's Word

Fill in the blanks.

1. The Lord called to Moses out of the ________________.
2. God said, "If you will keep My ________________, you shall be My treasured possession."
3. Then the Lord told Moses, "Go to the people and ____________________________ them."
4. All the people in the camp ________________________.
5. "I am the ______________ your God, who brought you out of the land of Egypt."
6. "I am a ______________________ God."
7. In six days, the Lord made heaven and earth and rested on the __________________________ day.

Thinking about God's Word

1. What did God promise to the Israelites if they kept his covenant?
2. With what signs did God show the people that He had something very serious and important to tell them?
3. Where did God take Moses to have him receive the Law?
4. Of what did God remind the Israelites before He gave the Ten Commandments?
5. What is the focus of the first three commandments?
6. What is the focus of the last seven commandments?
7. Which commandment comes with a promise, and what is that promise?

Applying God's Word

1. Are there any of the commandments that you haven't broken? See James 2:10.
2. God told the Israelites that if they kept His covenant they would be His "treasured possession . . . a kingdom of priests and a holy nation." Our sin has broken our relationship with God. But 1 Peter 1:9 says, "You are a chosen race, a royal priesthood, a holy nation, a people for His own possession." How is this possible?
3. Before giving the commandments, God said, "I am the LORD your God, who brought you out of the land of Egypt." How might God address us in light of our salvation in Christ? "I am the Lord your God, who . . ."

26

God's Covenant with the Israelites
(Exodus 32–34; 40)

Reviewing God's Word

Draw lines to match each word to its definition.

1. Consume	•Beg or plead
2. Implore	•Movable tent of worship
3. Relent	•Stubborn
4. Stiff-necked	•Formal, binding agreement
5. Pardon	•Destroy
6. Covenant	•Decide not to punish
7. Tabernacle	•Forgive or excuse

Thinking about God's Word

1. Why did the children of Israel become impatient with Moses?

2. What did the people start to worship instead of God?

3. What did God say to Moses when He saw the people worshiping an idol?

   What had God always called these people before?

4. What did God threaten to do?

5. What did God do when Moses begged Him to relent?

6. How did the people reply when God said He wouldn't go with them into the Promised Land?

   How did Moses reply?

7. What part of God was Moses allowed to see?

8. What did God in His goodness say when He passed by Moses?

9. How was Moses' appearance changed when he came down from the mountain?

10. How did God show that He had forgiven Israel and still claimed them as His people?

Applying God's Word

1. We often imitate the idolatry of our culture like the Israelites imitated the pagan culture around them. What gods do we make for ourselves?

2. Moses served as an intercessor between the people and God, pleading for their forgiveness. Who pleads before God in our defense?

3. God told Moses that man could not see Him without dying, and so He appeared to the people in various forms, including His "goodness," a cloud, and fire. What form did God take on when He came to earth to live?

   How does God come to us now?

27

The Twelve Spies (Numbers 13–14)

Reviewing God's Word

Underline the word or phrase that answers each question.

1. After how many days did the explorers return from Canaan? (25—30—40—50)
2. Which words show that the land was a good land? (grasshoppers—milk and honey—strongholds—camps)
3. Where did the people of Israel want to go? (Canaan—Egypt—wilderness—Cush)
4. What did Joshua and Caleb do in response to the people? (tore their clothes—gave in to the people—set out on their own—wept and moaned)
5. Who of the older Israelites would be allowed to enter Canaan? (Moses and Miriam—Joshua and Caleb—Aaron and Judah—Cain and Abel)
6. For how many years would the Israelites be punished for their sin? (25—75—50—40)

Thinking about God's Word

1. Why did God command Moses to send men into the land before the children of Israel went in?

2. When they returned, what did the explorers report to Moses?

   Why didn't they think the new land could be taken?

3. How did the Israelites respond?

4. How did they again show their lack of trust in God?

5. What did Joshua and Caleb tell the people?

6. After Moses pleaded with God not to disinherit the people, what did God say would be the punishment for their sin?

Applying God's Word

1. The spies reported all sorts of reasons why they couldn't enter Canaan: the cities were large and fortified, the people were strong, the people were huge. What things in your life do you feel are too big or too difficult for you to handle?

2. Describe Joshua and Caleb in the face of what many would consider an overwhelming obstacle.

   What confidence can you have in the face of overwhelming obstacles in your life?

3. How would the forty years in the wilderness remind the people of their sin? What knowledge of God's grace did the people possess during their forty years of wandering?

28

Water from a Rock and Fiery Serpents (Numbers 20–21)

Reviewing God's Word

Circle Yes or No for each statement.

1. The people of Israel grumbled against Moses, again.	YES	NO
2. Moses and Aaron brought their concern before the Lord.	YES	NO
3. God told Moses to strike the rock and bring forth water.	YES	NO
4. Moses followed God's instructions.	YES	NO
5. God gave the people water from the rock.	YES	NO
6. Moses and Aaron entered the Promised Land.	YES	NO
7. The people of Israel had no food to eat.	YES	NO
8. The people complained about the manna God had provided.	YES	NO
9. God sent fiery serpents to punish the people.	YES	NO
10. The people were saved from death by eating a special herb.	YES	NO

Thinking about God's Word

1. How did Moses and Aaron respond to the people's grumbling?

2. What were God's instructions to Moses and Aaron about getting water for the people?

3. What did Moses add to God's command?

4. Whom did Moses say would bring water from the rock?

5. Why was God upset with Moses and Aaron?

6. How did God punish the people for complaining again about food and water?

7. When Moses prayed for the people, how did God save the people from the serpents?

Applying God's Word

1. How do we sometimes act like the Israelites?

2. Who appeared as a serpent in the Garden of Eden in Genesis 3?

   How is he like the serpents in the wilderness?

3. The people of Israel were saved by a bronze snake that looked exactly like the serpents. How does this remind you of Jesus?

29

The Death of Moses
(Deuteronomy 18; 31; 34)

Reviewing God's Word

Underline the word or phrase that makes each sentence true.

1. Moses told the people that the practices of the Canaanite nations were (admirable—strange—abominable—God-pleasing).
2. God said the role of a prophet was to (make decisions—settle disputes—speak God's words—organize sacrifices).
3. (Caleb—Aaron—Joshua—Moses) was chosen by God to lead the children of Israel into Canaan.
4. It was up to (Joshua—God—the male warriors—the Israelites) to defeat the nations of Canaan.
5. God appeared to Moses and Joshua in the form of a(n) (pillar of cloud—angel—blazing fire—whirlwind).
6. (Joshua—The children of Israel—The LORD—Aaron) buried Moses.

Thinking about God's Word

1. What instruction did Moses give the people for their time in Canaan?
2. Whom did Moses promise that God would send?
3. What reasons did Moses give Joshua and the people for being "strong and courageous" as they entered the land?
4. How did the Lord show that Joshua was the leader He had chosen for His people?
5. What did the Lord show Moses from Mount Nebo before the prophet died?
6. Why did the Lord not permit His servant Moses to go into the Promised Land? See Numbers 20:7–12.
7. How did Joshua receive the spirit of wisdom?

Applying God's Word

1. Moses warned the people not to follow the ways of the unbelieving Canaanite people. What practices of unbelievers around us might be tempting to follow but displeasing to God?
2. What reason did Moses and God give for Joshua to be strong and courageous?

   How is this different from what the world says about courage?
3. Moses served as the leader of God's people for over forty years before he died. The Bible even says that no other prophet knew God face-to-face as Moses did. What comfort can we find in the fact that the Israelite nation still prospered after the death of Moses?

30

Rahab Hides the Spies (Joshua 1–2)

Reviewing God's Word

Write the name of the speaker next to each quote. Names may be used more than once.

1. "This Book of the Law shall not depart from your mouth."
2. "When the LORD gives us the land we will deal kindly and faithfully with you."
3. "Bring the men who have come to you. They have come to search out all the land."
4. "The LORD your God, He is God in the heavens above and on the earth beneath."
5. "Do not be frightened. Do not be dismayed."
6. "Truly the LORD has given all the land into our hands."
7. "View the land, especially Jericho."
8. "I know that the LORD has given you the land."

Joshua	God
The king of Jericho	The spies
Rahab	

Thinking about God's Word

1. What instructions did God give to Joshua?
2. Why did Joshua send out two men?
3. How did Rahab protect the spies?
4. How did Rahab show great faith?
5. Why were Rahab's actions so amazing?
6. What did Rahab ask for in exchange for protecting the spies?
7. How did the spies ask Rahab to identify her house?

Applying God's Word

1. How did God equip Joshua to lead Israel?

   How does God lead and equip us today?
2. How does the color of Rahab's cord remind you of how we have been saved?
3. Rahab believed in the Lord because she heard how He delivered the Israelites from the Egyptians. What does this mean about how we witness about God?

31

Israel Enters the Promised Land (Joshua 3–5)

Reviewing God's Word

God often used memorial markers or festivals as signs for people to remember His action in their lives and to teach their children about the Lord.

Draw lines to match each memorial with the event it commemorates. (See previous stories for hints.)

1. 12 stones at Gilgal	• God's promise to never again destroy the world by flood
2. Rainbows	• God preserving the firstborn children of Israel
3. Stone pillar at Bethel	• Jesus' death for the salvation of all people
4. Passover meal	• God's appearance to Jacob in a dream
5. Crosses	• The parting of the Jordan River

Thinking about God's Word

1. When the people were ready to cross the Jordan River and enter the Promised Land, who went first?

   What were the priests carrying?

2. What did the ark of the covenant show the Israelites?

3. How was it possible for the Israelites to pass through the Jordan River on dry ground?

4. Of what event from earlier in the history of Israel does this crossing remind you?

5. Why did the time of year make the parting of the Jordan River especially miraculous?

6. When did the waters of the Jordan flow as before?

7. What did Joshua do to commemorate the Israelites' entrance into the Promised Land?

8. Why did the manna stop falling from heaven?

9. Who appeared to Joshua near Jericho?

Applying God's Word

1. Joshua told the people to consecrate themselves because the Lord would do wonders among them. How are we made holy and set apart for God's use?

2. What parts of your church, like the stones in this account, help you remember what God has done for you?

3. The stones also served to teach the children about God's deliverance. How would you respond if someone asked you, "What does this cross mean?"

32

The Fall of Jericho (Joshua 6; 24)

Reviewing God's Word

Fill in the blanks.

1. "On the seventh day you shall march around the city ________________ times."
2. "Shout, for the LORD has ________________ you the city."
3. The spies brought out ________________ and all who belonged to her.
4. So ________________ was with Joshua, and his fame was in all the land.
5. "Fear the LORD. Serve Him in ________________ and in faithfulness."
6. "Choose this day whom you will ________________."
7. "It is the LORD our God who brought us and our fathers up from the land of ________________."

Thinking about God's Word

1. What was the first thing God said to Joshua as the Israelites approached Jericho?
2. How could God say this was already done when the walls hadn't fallen yet?
3. How did the children of Israel show their faith in God's plan to take Jericho?
4. What happened after the seventh day of marching when the people shouted and blew trumpets?
5. Why did Joshua tell the people to shout?
6. Why did God have the people walk in circles around the city instead of using conventional military tactics?
7. How did the Israelite spies keep their promise to Rahab?
8. Why did Joshua's fame spread throughout the land?
9. What choice did Joshua ask the people to make, and how did they respond?

Applying God's Word

1. God had won the victory for Israel before they even began marching. What victory has Christ already won for us?
2. Why was Rahab saved when God destroyed the city of Jericho?

   How are we delivered from God's punishment for sin?
3. Joshua told the people of Israel they needed to choose whom they were going to serve. How does this apply to you as well, and how is this choice connected to the First Commandment?

33

Deborah the Prophetess (Judges 2; 4–5)

Reviewing God's Word

Write the name of the speaker next to each quote. Names may be used more than once or not at all.

1. "Has not the LORD, the God of Israel, commanded you?"
2. "Turn aside to me. Do not be afraid."
3. "Hear, O kings. Give ear, O princes. To the LORD I will sing."
4. "If you [Deborah] will go with me, I will go."
5. "Up! For this is the day in which the LORD has given Sisera into your hand."
6. "Please give me a little water to drink."
7. "I will make melody to the LORD, the God of Israel."

Jael	Joshua
Jabin	Sisera
Deborah	Deborah and Barak
Barak	

Thinking about God's Word

1. Why were the Israelites under the control of Jabin, king of Canaan?
2. Who was the judge over Israel at this time?
3. What had God already commanded Barak to do?
4. Why hadn't Barak followed God's command yet?
5. What did Deborah tell Barak would be his punishment for not trusting God to be with him and deliver him?
6. How did Israel win the battle?
7. What did Sisera do to try to escape being killed?
8. How did God bring to pass what Deborah had predicted?
9. What did Deborah and Barak do after the victory?

Applying God's Word

1. The text says that the people of Israel didn't know the Lord and did what was evil in His sight. How are these two things related?
2. Barak was frightened and doubtful about God's promise to defeat Sisera. When have you felt a similar fear? What comfort can you find in this account?
3. How are the songs of praise we sing to God like the song of Barak and Deborah?

34

Gideon Defeats Midian
(Judges 6–8)

Reviewing God's Word

Underline the word or phrase that answers each question.

1. Into whose hands did the Lord give Israel? (Philistia—Egypt—Ammon—Midian)
2. Who came to Gideon? (Deborah—The elders of Israel—The angel of the Lord—The king)
3. About what did Gideon ask the angel as evidence that God was present with Israel? (Wonderful deeds—The Lord Himself—An army of angels—A vision from God)
4. How many men were used by God to defeat the Midianites? (22,000—300—32,000—10,000)
5. When did Gideon and his men go to the camp of Midian? (Noon—Morning—Night—Afternoon)
6. Who caused the Midianites to turn on one another? (Gideon—The Israelite army—Midian—God)

Thinking about God's Word

1. How does the opening of this story remind you of the beginning of the story of Deborah the Prophetess?

2. Why did Gideon have trouble believing that God was with Israel?

3. With what was Gideon clothed?

4. Why did the Lord reduce Gideon's army from 32,000 men to 300 men?

5. What tactic did Gideon's men use?

6. How did the LORD give Israel victory?

7. In the words of their battle cry, how did Gideon's men show that they believed God would help them?

Applying God's Word

1. Gideon doubted God's presence because he hadn't seen the "wonderful deeds" he expected from God. What is the most wonderful deed that God has done to assure us completely of His presence among us? See Matthew 1:23.

2. Gideon was clothed with the Spirit of the LORD. With what were you clothed in your Baptism?

3. In the New Testament, 1 Corinthians 1:25 records, "For the foolishness of God is wiser than man's wisdom, and the weakness of God is stronger than men." How does this Old Testament account exemplify the truth of these New Testament words?

35

God Makes Samson Strong (Judges 13; 15–16)

Reviewing God's Word

Fill in the blanks, using the words below. Some words will not be used.

1. Samson's work was to begin to save ________________ from the Philistines.
2. The ______________ of the LORD gave Samson strength.
3. Samson fell in love with ________________________.
4. The ____________ of the Philistines told Delilah to find the secret of Samson's strength.
5. When Samson lost his __________, he lost his strength.
6. The Philistines sacrificed to ____________________.
7. Samson's ___________________________ buried him.

Delilah	The Lord	Spirit
commanders	shirt	friends
Dagon	lords	Israel

Thinking about God's Word

1. Why did the LORD give Israel over to the Philistines?

2. What message did the angel of the LORD bring to Manoah's wife?

3. What miraculous thing did God empower Samson to do when the men of Judah bound him?

4. What did the Philistines want Delilah to find out for them about Samson?

5. What was the secret of his strength?

6. What did the Philistines do to Samson?

7. How do you know the Philistines didn't worship the Lord?

8. Who gave Samson the strength to bring down the house of the Philistines?

Applying God's Word

1. What pattern are you noticing in these stories from Judges?

   How is this like us?

2. How did the Philistines break the First Commandment? How did Samson break the First Commandment?

   What people or things are you tempted to put before God?

3. Compare Samson with Jesus, the ultimate Deliverer.

36

Ruth
(The Book of Ruth)

Reviewing God's Word

Circle Yes or No for each statement.

1. Naomi was from Moab.	YES	NO
2. Naomi wanted Orpah and Ruth to return to Judah with her.	YES	NO
3. Ruth insisted on going with Naomi.	YES	NO
4. Boaz was from Bethlehem.	YES	NO
5. Ruth stole from the field of Boaz.	YES	NO
6. Boaz praised Ruth for the way she had taken care of Naomi.	YES	NO
7. Boaz was a family redeemer who took care of Naomi and Ruth.	YES	NO
8. Ruth was an ancestor of King David.	YES	NO

Thinking about God's Word

1. Why did Elimelech and his family go to Moab?

2. Whom did Elimelech's sons marry?

3. What happened to Naomi's family?

4. How does the narrative describe the end of the famine?

5. How did Ruth answer when Naomi told her daughters-in-law to return to their own homes while she went back to Judah?

6. Why must it have been difficult for Ruth to go with Naomi?

7. How did Ruth provide for Naomi?

8. What blessing did Boaz speak to Ruth?

9. Why did Naomi send Ruth to Boaz?

10. What did Boaz do in addition to buying the land?

Applying God's Word

1. How was Boaz like Christ?

2. How did Ruth show through her actions the connection between faith and loving service toward others?

3. Every single person we meet is someone for whom Christ died. Boaz went above and beyond the law to care for and provide for Ruth and Naomi. What can we learn from His example?

37

Hannah and Samuel
(1 Samuel 1–2)

Reviewing God's Word

Draw a line through the sentences that are not true.

1. Elkanah had a wife by the name of Hannah.
2. Peninnah was the wife of Elkanah.
3. Peninnah had pity on Hannah.
4. Hannah made a vow to the LORD .
5. Hannah was drunk when she prayed in the temple.
6. Hannah named her son Eli.
7. Hannah kept her vow to the Lord.

Thinking about God's Word

Answer each question.

1. Why was Hannah so upset that she wept and didn't eat?

2. What did Hannah do about her problem?

3. What vow did Hannah make to the LORD?

4. How did the LORD remember Hannah?

5. How did Hannah keep her promise to the LORD?

6. How else did Hannah thank God for His gift of Samuel?

Applying God's Word

1. Hannah describes her prayer as "pouring out [her] soul before the LORD." God wants us to tell Him about all our pain, excitement, worry, distress, and joy, and He promises to hear all our prayers. What joys or sorrows can you share with God today?

   Take a moment and pour out your soul in prayer.

2. Hannah realized that Samuel was a gift from God, and so she gave him to the LORD to serve in His house. What gifts has God given you that you can use to serve in His kingdom?

3. The birth of Samuel was a sign for Hannah and Elkanah of God's grace. What special baby was born a thousand years later as a perfect expression of God's grace?

38

God Calls Samuel
(1 Samuel 2–4)

Reviewing God's Word

Draw lines to match each word to its definition.

1. Perceive	• To mock and show a lack or respect for God
2. Blaspheme	• To hold back from action
3. Minister	• To serve by fulfilling priestly duties
4. Restrain	• To realize

Thinking about God's Word

1. Why does the account say Eli's sons were worthless?

2. Who did Samuel think was calling him when he heard his name?

3. Who was really calling Samuel?

4. What did Samuel say when he realized the LORD was calling him?

5. What did God tell Samuel?

6. What was Eli's response when he heard what was going to happen?

7. How did God bring about the punishment He had promised?

8. What did the Philistines capture in battle?

Applying God's Word

1. The Bible says that Samuel did not yet know the Lord because the Word of the Lord hadn't been revealed to him. How do we come to know God?

2. What can we learn from Samuel's example about how to respond to God's Word?

3. Samuel heard the voice of the LORD call out, "Samuel!" When did God call you by name to know Him and be His child?

39

Saul Becomes King (1 Samuel 8–11)

Reviewing God's Word

Of whom do you think when you read each of the following sentences?

1. The elders of Israel came to speak to him.
2. He chose the man to be anointed as king.
3. He was the son of Kish and the first king of Israel.
4. They shouted, "Long live the king!"
5. He hid among the baggage.
6. He led the people to defeat the Ammonites.
7. He said, "Let us renew the kingdom."

Saul	God	Samuel
Benjamin	Kish	People of Israel

Thinking about God's Word

1. Why did the elders tell Samuel they wanted a king?

2. Why was it a sin to ask for a king?

3. How did God use natural events to send Saul to Samuel?

4. What did God promise that Saul would do?

5. Why were the people so impressed with Saul?

6. How did God bless Saul in battle?

7. What two things did the Israelites do to celebrate their victory in battle and renew the kingdom?

Applying God's Word

1. What does this account teach us about the relationship between God and our governing authorities?

   What does this account teach us about how we treat our rulers?

2. Saul was in the midst of an ordinary search for lost donkeys when God led Samuel to anoint him king of Israel. What does this occurrence suggest about the ordinary moments of your life?

3. Saul was the first in a line of kings who were supposed to lead and deliver the people of Israel, but no king was able to do this perfectly. Whom did God ultimately send to lead and deliver His people?

40

Samuel Anoints David (1 Samuel 15–16)

Reviewing God's Word

Write the name of the speaker next to each quote. Names may be used more than once or not at all.

1. "Why did you not obey the voice of the LORD?"
2. "Do not look on his appearance."
3. "There remains yet the youngest. He is keeping the sheep."
4. "I have sinned. Please pardon my sin and return with me."
5. "I regret that I have made Saul king."
6. "You have rejected the word of the LORD, and the LORD has rejected you from being king over Israel."
7. "Strike Amalek and destroy all that they have. Do not spare them."

David	Jesse	Eliab
Saul	God	Samuel

Thinking about God's Word

1. In what way did Saul disobey God after defeating the Amalekites?
2. Why did God regret making Saul king?
3. Why did Samuel refuse to excuse Saul's sin and return with him?
4. Why did the Lord send Samuel to Jesse?
5. Where did Jesse and his family live?
6. What did God tell Samuel when Samuel was sure Eliab was the Lord's choice for the next king?
7. Whom had God chosen to be king?

Applying God's Word

1. In disobedience to God's command, Saul and his men greedily kept the best spoils for themselves. When have you acted selfishly in your use of God's gifts to you?
2. The LORD says that He looks at the heart. What is the condition of our hearts?
3. What similarities can you already see between David and Jesus?

41

David Fights Goliath
(1 Samuel 17)

Reviewing God's Word

Underline the word or phrase that answers each question.

1. Whom were the Israelites fighting against in this story?
   (Amalekites—Midianites—Philistines—Bethlehemites)
2. Who had followed Saul to battle?
   (David—Jesse's three oldest sons—Saul's brothers—Jesse)
3. From what had the LORD already delivered David?
   (Lions and bears—Many armies—Deadly disease—A poisonous serpent)
4. What did Saul try to give David?
   (Money—A javelin—A sling—His armor)
5. How did David kill Goliath?
   (With a spear—With a sling and a stone—With a curse—With an army)
6. Whose battle was this?
   (Saul's—Goliath's—The Lord's—David's)

Thinking about God's Word

1. What kind of battle did Goliath call for?
2. Why were the Israelites so afraid to fight?
3. Why did David go to the battlefield in the first place?
4. With what words did David show that he was not frightened by the giant?
5. Why was David willing to fight Goliath?
6. What did David take with him to fight the giant?
7. With what did Goliath arm himself?
8. Who did David say would deliver Israel?
9. How did David kill Goliath?
10. What happened when the Philistines saw that Goliath was dead?

Applying God's Word

1. God told Paul, "My grace is sufficient for you, for My power is made perfect in weakness" (2 Corinthians 12:9). How does the account of David and Goliath demonstrate this?
2. How does it change our attitude toward our own weaknesses to know that God's power is made perfect in weakness?
3. What can we learn from David about facing difficulties and battles in our own lives?

42

David and Jonathan
(1 Samuel 18; 20)

Reviewing God's Word

Fill in the blanks.

1. The soul of Jonathan, Saul's son, was ____________ to the soul of David.
2. But as David won battles, Saul sought to __________ him.
3. David said of Saul, "If he is ________________, then know that he is determined to harm me."
4. Saul said to Jonathan, "For as long as the son of Jesse lives on the earth, neither you nor your ___________________ shall be established."
5. Jonathan knew that his _______________ was determined to put David to death.
6. Jonathan said to David, "The LORD shall be between me and you, and between my offspring and your offspring, ____________________________."

Thinking about God's Word

1. Who was Jonathan?
2. Who usually takes over the throne when a king dies?
3. Whom had Samuel already anointed to be king after Saul? (See previous two stories.)
4. How does the Bible describe the way Jonathan loved his friend David?
5. When did Saul begin trying to kill David?
6. How did Jonathan test his father to find out his attitude toward David?
7. What reason did Saul give when he told Jonathan he was going to kill David?
8. With what action did Jonathan tell David that he needed to flee from Saul?
9. Who was at the center of Jonathan and David's friendship?

Applying God's Word

1. Jesus taught that the second greatest commandment is "You shall love your neighbor as yourself" (Matthew 22:39). How did Jonathan follow this command?
2. The name Jonathan means "gift of God." Truly, Saul's son was a gift of blessing and protection for David. What people in your life are God's gifts to you?
3. God had promised Abraham that kings would come from his descendants. How does this account show God at work to keep His promise?

43

God's Covenant with David (2 Samuel 7)

Reviewing God's Word

Circle Yes or No for each statement.

1. David had a permanent dwelling, while the Israelites worshiped in a tent.	YES	NO
2. The Lord told David to make Him a temple.	YES	NO
3. David rose from a shepherd to a king through hard work and determination.	YES	NO
4. The Lord promised to give the throne to David's offspring.	YES	NO
5. God said David's son would build the temple as a house for the Lord.	YES	NO
6. The Lord promised that David's throne would be established forever.	YES	NO
7. God said David's son would follow His commands perfectly.	YES	NO
8. David went into the tabernacle tent and praised God for all His blessings.	YES	NO

Thinking about God's Word

1. How did God bless David in battle?

2. Why did David go to Nathan the prophet?

3. What did the LORD say He had done for David?

4. What did God promise to do for David's son?

5. What did the Lord say He would do when David's son sinned?

6. Did God bless David because David was a really good person?

7. What did David say about why the Lord had given him greatness?

Applying God's Word

1. Who in this account did all the action: made David king, brought an end to battle, gave Israel a place to live, established David's kingdom, promised to bring success to David's son?

   What does this mean for the events of our lives?

2. What does this account teach us about why God gives us blessings?

3. God promised that He would establish David's throne forever. Who is reigning on David's throne today?

44

Solomon Becomes King (1 Kings 2–3)

Reviewing God's Word

Draw lines to match each quote to the person who spoke it. More than one quote may be matched with the same speaker.

1. "Keep the charge of the LORD your God, walking in His ways."
2. "I give you a wise and discerning mind."
3. "Who is able to govern this Your great people?"
4. "I give you also riches and honor."
5. "Be strong. Show yourself a man."
6. "I am but a little child. Your servant is in the midst of Your people."
7. "If you will walk in My ways . . . then I will lengthen your days."

• Solomon

• God

• David

Thinking about God's Word

1. What commands did David give his son Solomon before he died?
2. What does it mean that David "slept with his fathers"?
3. What did the Lord say to Solomon when He appeared to him in a dream?
4. For what did Solomon ask the Lord?
5. What did God give Solomon in addition to wisdom?
6. What did Solomon do when he awoke?
7. Why did two women come to Solomon?
8. What was Solomon's solution to their conflict?
9. Why were the people amazed at Solomon?

Applying God's Word

1. What does it mean to walk in the Lord's ways? How do we know what God's ways are?
2. How is it possible to walk in the Lord's ways?
3. Where does the world say wisdom comes from? Where does true wisdom come from?

45

Solomon Builds the Temple
(1 Kings 5–6; 8)

Reviewing God's Word

Underline the word or phrase that answers each question.

1. Whom did Solomon ask to provide cedar and cypress wood? (The tribe of Judah —The tribe of Benjamin—The Egyptians—Hiram, king of Tyre)
2. How many years had Israel been out of Egypt before Solomon began building the temple? (200—77—480—600)
3. With what did Solomon cover the altar in the inner sanctuary? (Gold—Nickel—Copper—Silver)
4. How many years did Solomon spend building the temple? (10–12—2—7)
5. Where was the ark of the covenant placed? (In the palace—In the Most Holy Place—In the court—In the courtyard)
6. By what name did Solomon call God in his prayer? (Jehovah—God—Almighty—Lord, God of Israel)
7. What specifically did Solomon ask God to do in the very end of his prayer? (Give all the people wisdom—Grant Israel wealth—Defeat his enemies—Forgive the people)

Thinking about God's Word

1. What deal did Solomon make with Hiram, king of Tyre?

2. What was the wonderful result of this treaty?

3. How did the temple demonstrate Solomon's love for God?

4. How did God show that He was present in the temple?

5. What did Solomon do to dedicate the temple?

Applying God's Word

1. Solomon acknowledged that even heaven couldn't contain God, yet God chose to be present in the temple. How do we know that God is present with us in worship?

2. What can you learn from Solomon about how to view your church?

3. Solomon said to the Lord, "Listen in heaven Your dwelling place, and when You hear, forgive." How can we be certain that when God hears our prayers He will forgive our sins?

46

God Provides for Elijah (1 Kings 16–17)

Reviewing God's Word

Fill in the blanks, using the words below. Some words will not be used.

1. Ahab sinned against God by worshiping ______________.
2. ____________________ the prophet told Ahab there would be years with neither dew nor rain.
3. ______________________ brought Elijah bread and meat.
4. The Lord told Elijah to go to the city of ______________.
5. God used a ________________________ to care for Elijah.
6. After some time, the widow's __________________ died.
7. ________________ brought the widow's child back to life.

Zarephath	Elijah	Baal
daughter	maiden	Ahab
Dogs	The Lord	Ravens
widow	son	Samaria

Thinking about God's Word

1. What did Ahab do that showed he was a wicked king?
2. What did the Lord do to call Ahab to repentance?
3. Why was having "neither dew nor rain" a terrible punishment?
4. How did the Lord miraculously take care of Elijah?
5. Why did Elijah go to Zarephath?
6. Why was it unusual for God to command a widow to feed Elijah?
7. Why did Elijah tell the widow not to be afraid?
8. How did the widow show that she believed God would provide?
9. What tragedy happened while Elijah was staying with the widow?
10. How did God provide in this situation too?

Applying God's Word

1. In this account, what powerful things did the Lord do by His Word?

   What power does the Word of the Lord (the Bible) have in your life?

2. How does God's care for Elijah compare with God's care for us?

3. What other Bible accounts show God's power over death?

   What does God's power over death mean for us?

47

Elijah and the Prophets of Baal

(1 Kings 18)

Reviewing God's Word

Draw a line through the sentences that are not true.

1. Elijah told King Ahab to gather 450 prophets of Baal and 400 prophets of Asherah.
2. Elijah proposed a contest to see who the true god was.
3. The prophets called to Dagon to bring down fire.
4. A voice called from heaven to the prophets of Baal.
5. Elijah built an altar with twelve stones.
6. Elijah tried to make it easier for the bull on his altar to burn.
7. God sent fire to consume the offering, the wood, the stones, the water, and the dust.
8. After God sent fire for His altar, the people worshiped the Lord.
9. The prophets of Baal repented and believed in God.

Thinking about God's Word

1. Whom were the people worshiping besides God?

2. How did Elijah put the idol Baal to a test?

3. What showed that the idol Baal had no power?

4. What did the twelve stones of Elijah's altar represent?

5. Why did Elijah drench his altar with water?

6. How can you tell that the fire that fell from heaven was sent by God?

7. With what action and words did the people confess that Elijah had won the test?

8. What did the people do with the prophets of Baal at Elijah's command?

Applying God's Word

1. Elijah asked the people how long they would "limp between two different opinions." God wants us to love Him with all our heart, soul, and mind (Matthew 22:37). What things in your life steal some of your trust and focus?

2. Elijah mocked the prophets of Baal by asking them if their god was sleeping and needed to be woken up. Why do we never have to worry about the true God needing to be awoken?

3. Elijah prayed to the God of Abraham, Isaac, and Israel. Is Elijah's God the same as ours? Explain.

48

God Takes Elijah to Heaven (1 Kings 19; 2 Kings 2)

Reviewing God's Word

Underline the word or phrase that makes each sentence true.

1. After Elijah killed the prophets of Baal, (Ahab—Elisha—Asherah—Jezebel) threatened to kill him.
2. Elijah traveled forty days to Mount (Sinai—Horeb—Carmel—Shepher).
3. God spoke to Elijah in a (whisper—wind—earthquake—fire).
4. Elijah asked Elisha to (follow him—lead him—stay behind—wander), but Elisha refused.
5. Elisha asked for a (single—triple—half—double) portion of Elijah's spirit.
6. Elisha called Elijah his (brother—friend—father—master).
7. Elisha used Elijah's (shoe—cloak—staff—scroll) to part the Jordan River.

Thinking about God's Word

1. Why did Elijah run into the wilderness?
2. How did Elijah get food and water?
3. How did God come to Elijah?
4. Why did Elijah seek out the Lord?
5. What did the Lord tell Elijah to do?
6. How did Elijah and Elisha cross the Jordan?
7. What did Elisha ask for from his teacher Elijah before he took over as prophet?
8. How was Elijah taken up into heaven?
9. By what miracle did the Lord show Elisha that He was with him as He had been with Elijah?

Applying God's Word

1. When Elijah felt completely discouraged and alone, God sent him Elisha to assist him and learn from him. What other Christians has God placed in your life to remind you that you aren't the only one left?
2. How do you know that you have received the Holy Spirit? See 1 Corinthians 12:3.
3. When Elijah went up on the mountain to wait for the Lord to pass by, God wasn't in the wind, earthquake, or fire, but He was in a low whisper. How does God show Himself to you in seemingly quiet and insignificant ways?

49

Naaman and Elisha

(2 Kings 5)

Reviewing God's Word

Write the name of the speaker next to each quote. Names may be used more than once or not at all.

1. "Let Naaman come to me, that he may know that there is a prophet in Israel."
2. "It is a great word the prophet has spoken to you."
3. "Go now, and I will send a letter to the king of Israel."
4. "Are not the rivers of Damascus better than all the waters of Israel?
5. "Am I God, to kill and to make alive?"
6. "Go in peace."
7. "Would that my lord were with the prophet who is in Samaria!"
8. "Behold, I know that there is no God in all the earth but in Israel."

Naaman	Elijah	Elisha
Kind of Syria	Naaman's servants	Jezebel
King of Israel	Baal	Israelite servant girl

Thinking about God's Word

1. Who was Naaman?
2. What was wrong with him?
3. What did the servant girl say?
4. Why did the king of Israel tear his clothes?
5. How did Elisha humble Naaman?
6. Why was Naaman upset?
7. What happened when Naaman followed Elisha's instructions?
8. With what words did Naaman admit that God of Israel had cured him?
9. Why do you think Elisha refused Naaman's present?

Applying God's Word

1. How did the servant girl act as a missionary?
2. What evidence does the witness of the servant girl provide of God's love and grace for all people?
3. Naaman was upset that he had to wash in the Jordan River rather than the waters of Damascus, but his servants said to him, "It is a great word the prophet has spoken to you." Where did the power come from for Naaman's healing? How is this like Baptism?

50

Jonah
(The Book of Jonah)

Reviewing God's Word

Fill in the blanks.

1. The ____________________ of the Lord came to Jonah.

2. Jonah found a ship going to ____________________, away from the presence of the Lord.

3. The mariners were afraid, and each cried out to his ________________________________.

4. Jonah said, "I am a Hebrew. I fear the LORD, the God of ________________________________."

5. The sailors hurled Jonah into the ________________, and the sea ceased its raging.

6. The Lord appointed a great ______________ to swallow up Jonah.

7. "When my life was fainting away, I ______________ the LORD."

8. The people of Nineveh ______________________ God.

9. God ____________________ of the disaster that He had said He would do to the people of Nineveh.

Thinking about God's Word

1. What did the Lord tell Jonah to do?

2. What did Jonah do instead?

3. What did the sailors do when God sent a great storm?

4. What did Jonah tell the sailors to do when they discovered he had caused the storm by trying to run away from God?

5. How did God use Jonah's disobedience to bring other people to faith?

6. How did God show mercy to Jonah?

7. How long was Jonah in the belly of the fish?

8. What did Jonah do while he was in the belly of the fish?

9. What did the people of Nineveh do when they heard Jonah's message?

10. How did God respond to their repentance?

Applying God's Word

1. Do you ever try to avoid doing what you know God wants you to do?

   What did Jonah learn about running away from God?

2. The people of Nineveh seemed completely lost in their sin, but God worked repentance and faith in their hearts. When have you assumed people are too lost to be worth witnessing to?

   Why is it that no one is too lost for the Gospel?

3. How is God's salvation for the people of Nineveh like the salvation He offers to us?

51

Isaiah Sees the Lord (Isaiah 6–7; 9; 53)

Reviewing God's Word

Draw lines to match each word to its definition.

1. Seraphim	• To hold someone in high regard
2. Atone	• Sins
3. Immanuel	• Six-winged angels created by God
4. Esteem	• Punishment
5. Smitten	• Name of Jesus, means "God is with us"
6. Transgressions	• To pay for
7. Chastisement	• Struck, as with a hard blow

Thinking about God's Word

1. How did Isaiah describe the LORD, as he saw Him in his vision?

2. What did the seraphim call out?

3. What did the seraphim do after flying to Isaiah?

4. How did Isaiah answer when God asked whom He should send?

5. What kind of sign did God promise to Israel?

6. What other names did God give for the promised Savior?

7. According to the last prophecy, what terrible things would Jesus have to suffer and what good things would His suffering mean for us?

Applying God's Word

1. Isaiah had to have his sins taken away before he was ready to worship God or serve as God's messenger. How do we follow his example in our church services?

2. Isaiah gave five names for Jesus: Immanuel, Wonderful Counselor, Mighty God, Everlasting Father, and Prince of Peace. What does each of these names tell us about God?

3. Why did Jesus suffer in the brutal way Isaiah describes? And what does this suffering mean for us?

52

King Hezekiah Prays
(2 Kings 18–19)

Reviewing God's Word

Circle Yes or No for each statement.

1. Hezekiah followed the Lord's commands as king of Israel.	YES	NO
2. Sennacherib was the powerful king of Assyria.	YES	NO
3. All the cities of Judah were able to fight off the Assyrian army.	YES	NO
4. Hezekiah gave Sennacherib the silver and gold he requested.	YES	NO
5. The Assyrians respected and worshiped the Lord.	YES	NO
6. After the Assyrians' taunting, Hezekiah went into the house of the Lord.	YES	NO
7. Isaiah told Hezekiah that there was no hope for Jerusalem.	YES	NO
8. The army of Israel fought and defeated the Assyrians.	YES	NO

Thinking about God's Word

1. How was Hezekiah a good king?

2. Why did Hezekiah give silver and gold to the king of Assyria?

3. What did the leaders of the Assyrian army tell the people of Jerusalem?

4. What did the Lord tell Isaiah to say to Hezekiah?

5. What did Hezekiah do when he received another threatening letter from Sennacherib?

6. What did God promise to Hezekiah?

7. How did the Lord keep His promise to deliver Jerusalem?

Applying God's Word

1. How can we find comfort in this account when we face problems that seem unbeatable?

2. What can we learn from Hezekiah about how to handle troubling situations?

3. Hezekiah asked God to save Jerusalem "that all the kingdoms of the earth may know that You, O Lord, are God alone." How can this serve as a model for our prayers?

53

King Josiah (2 Kings 22–23)

Reviewing God's Word

Underline the word or phrase that makes each sentence true.

1. Josiah was only (12—10—8—9) years old when he became king.
2. The high priest when Josiah was king was (Hilkiah—Huldah—Asherah—David).
3. Josiah was (amused—repentant—angry—unconcerned) when he heard the words of the Book of the Law.
4. The Lord said He would bring disaster on Judah because the people had (not celebrated the Passover—taken too long repairing the temple—worshiped other gods—made Josiah king).
5. King Josiah commanded the people to celebrate the (Passover—Feast of Weeks—Day of Atonement—Feast of Booths).

Thinking about God's Word

1. What does it mean that Josiah walked in the way of King David?
2. What did King Josiah want done with the offerings collected from the people?
3. What did Hilkiah find in the house of the LORD?
4. What did Josiah do when he heard the Book of the Law read aloud?
5. Why was Josiah so upset?
6. What message did Huldah the prophetess give to Josiah from the LORD?
7. Then to whom did Josiah read the Book of the Law?
8. What covenant did the people make before the LORD?
9. What specific things did Josiah do to return the nation to following the LORD?

Applying God's Word

1. Josiah did what was right in God's eyes, even as a young boy, by walking in the way of David and following the guidance of Hilkiah. Whom has God placed in your life to give you a godly example and godly instruction to follow?
2. A wide variety of people were used to repair the temple, including carpenters, builders, and masons. What does this suggest about how God would have us understand and use our jobs and abilities?
3. What comfort can we find in the Lord's response to Josiah's repentance?

54

God Calls Jeremiah (Jeremiah 1; 23; 31)

Reviewing God's Word

Match each prophecy with its fulfillment by writing the correct letter next to each numbered statement.

1. God would give Jeremiah words to speak.______
2. God would use Jeremiah to break down and destroy and to build up and plant. _____
3. God would send a righteous Branch of David.______
4. The Lord would be a shepherd to Israel.______
5. God would make a new covenant with His people.______
6. The Lord would forgive His peoples' sins.______

a. Jesus said, "I am the good shepherd" (John 10:11).

b. Jesus was born of David's descendants and lived a perfect, righteous life.

c. Jeremiah wrote two books (57 chapters) of the Bible.

d. Jesus died and rose again to pay for the sins of all people.

e. Jesus' blood sealed a new covenant and brought us peace with God (1 Corinthians 11:25).

f. Jeremiah prophesied God's judgment on the Israelites (Jeremiah 1–29; 34–52) and God's restoration of His people through Jesus Christ (Jeremiah 30–33).

Thinking about God's Word

1. What did the LORD tell Jeremiah He had appointed him to be?

2. Why did Jeremiah think he couldn't do what God had asked?

3. What two promises did God make to Jeremiah to reassure him and calm his fears?

4. How did the LORD show Jeremiah that the words he prophesied would be straight from God?

5. How did the LORD describe the "righteous Branch" of David?

6. What other name did the LORD give Jeremiah for this "righteous Branch"?

7. God promised to be a loving shepherd to His people. Then how did He promise to transform the people?

8. What did the LORD promise about His Law?

9. And what did God promise to do about the people's sins?

Applying God's Word

1. The Lord told Jeremiah that before he was born (and even before He formed him in the womb) He set Jeremiah apart for a specific purpose. What does this mean about how we view the life of an unborn child?

2. Do you ever say to God "I'm only a youth" or "I'm only a kid"?

   How does the account of Jeremiah assure you that you're never too young to serve the Lord?

3. To be righteous means to be right with God. If another name for Jesus is "the LORD is our righteousness," how do we enter into a right relationship with God?

55

Israel and Judah in Exile (2 Kings 17; 24–25)

Reviewing God's Word

Fill in the blanks, using the words and numbers below. Some words will not be used.

1. Hoshea was king over ____________________.
2. God used the nation of ________________ to bring judgment on Israel.
3. The Israelites had ignored the warnings God gave through the ____________________.
4. Jehoiachin was an evil king of ________________.
5. Judah was taken into captivity by ________________ as a result of God's judgment.
6. ________________ was blinded, bound, and taken into exile.
7. The king of Babylon freed Zedekiah from prison after ________ years of exile.

Judah	Zedekiah	Josiah
Jerusalem	55	scribes
Assyria	Babylon	prophets
kings	Israel	37

Thinking about God's Word

1. What was Hoshea like as a king?

2. Why did God let the Assyrians carry the Israelites into captivity?

3. In what way did God warn Israel and Judah about their sin and the exile that would occur as a judgment against their sin?

4. How does the account describe Jehoiachin as a king?

5. What did Nebuchadnezzar and the Babylonians do to Judah?

6. In what way was Zedekiah like Hoshea and Jehoiachin?

7. What happened as a result of Zedekiah's sin and God's further judgment on Judah?

8. How did the king of Babylon show kindness to Jehoiachin?

Applying God's Word

1. What does this account tell us about God's attitude toward sin?

2. Since God is just and cannot tolerate sin, our sin requires punishment as well. Why will we not receive the punishment, exile, and death we deserve?

3. God showed mercy and patience toward Israel by warning the people over and over to repent and turn from their sin. How does God show mercy and patience with unbelievers now? See 2 Peter 3:9.

56

God's Promises to the Exiles (Ezekiel 8; 36)

Reviewing God's Word

Draw a line through the sentences that are not true.

1. The people of Israel were committing great abominations.
2. God left the temple.
3. God refused to punish Israel's sin because they were His people.
4. The Israelites had acted just like the sinful nations around them.
5. Once the Israelites were exiled, God had forsaken them forever.
6. God told the Israelites to fix their own hearts of stone.
7. God promised to give the Israelites His Spirit.
8. The Lord promised to restore Israel to a land like the Garden of Eden.

Thinking about God's Word

1. What drove God from the temple?
2. How would the LORD act toward His people in their sin?
3. What did Ezekiel see in a vision that showed God's judgment on Israel?
4. What was the LORD's purpose in giving Israel over to foreign nations?
5. How would the LORD later show all the nations that He is God?
6. What two things did God say He would use to cleanse His people, renew their hearts, and restore them to a life of following His commandments?
7. How did the Lord describe the new land He would give to Israel?
8. What did God say to assure Ezekiel that these prophecies would really happen?

Applying God's Word

1. The LORD told Ezekiel that He was exiling the people in hope that they would repent and realize He is God. How does this help make sense of some of the difficult things you go through?
2. How does God bring us the sprinkling with water and gift of the Spirit that He promised in Ezekiel?
3. Do you ever wonder how we can know that God will keep His promises to be with us always, to forgive our sins, and to take us to heaven when we die?

   What comfort do you find in God's final words to Ezekiel?

57

The Three Men in the Fiery Furnace (Daniel 3)

Reviewing God's Word

Draw lines to match each quote to a speaker. Names may match more than one quote.

1. "Blessed be the God of Shadrach, Meshach, and Abednego."
2. "When you hear the music, you are to fall down and worship."
3. "Our God whom we serve is able to deliver us."
4. "Who is the god who will deliver you out of my hands?"
5. "These men, O king, pay no attention to you."
6. "O king, we will not serve your gods or worship the golden image."

- The herald
- The Chaldeans
- Nebuchadnezzar
- Shadrach, Meshach, and Abednego

Thinking about God's Word

1. How did Nebuchadnezzar sin against the First Commandment?
2. How did the king force the people to commit idolatry?
3. What punishment did the king use to threaten the people if they refused to worship the idol?
4. Who did not obey the command of the king?
5. What did Shadrach, Meshach, and Abednego say when Nebuchadnezzar threatened to throw them into the furnace?
6. How do we know the furnace was very hot?
7. Why was Nebuchadnezzar astonished?
8. How did Nebuchadnezzar and the people know that God had completely protected the three men?
9. How did the king change as a result of this event?

Applying God's Word

1. When the music played, "all the people" bowed down and worshiped the idol. Shadrach, Meshach, and Abednego could have used the excuse that "everyone is doing it," but they chose to follow God instead. What sinful things does it seem like "everyone is doing," and how can you bring God glory by following Him instead?
2. God didn't stop Shadrach, Meshach, and Abednego from entering the fire, but He did save them while they were in the fire. What does this suggest about difficult times in our lives?
3. Why did Shadrach, Meshach, and Abednego say they would still love and thank God even if He didn't rescue them from the furnace?

58

Daniel in the Lions' Den (Daniel 6)

Reviewing God's Word

Underline the word or phrase that makes each sentence true.

1. The king made Daniel (a servant—a king—a prince—a president) in the land.
2. The king signed (an ordinance—a book—a petition—a dominion).
3. It said that no one was to pray to anyone except (God—the king—Daniel—the princes) for thirty days.
4. Daniel prayed (10—3—20—5) times a day.
5. The king let Daniel be thrown to the lions because he (wanted Daniel killed—could not change the law—hated Daniel—wished to please the princes).

Thinking about God's Word

1. How did Daniel become distinguished in the land?

2. Why did the presidents and satraps want to get Daniel in trouble?

3. What ordinance did the presidents and satraps persuade the king to sign?

4. How did the new law appeal to the king's pride and at the same time break the First Commandment?

5. How did Daniel respond to the ordinance?

6. Who reported Daniel's worship to the king?

7. How can you tell that the king thought highly of Daniel?

8. How did God protect Daniel?

9. What happened to the men who had tried to get Daniel killed?

Applying God's Word

1. Daniel's godly actions and constant prayer caught the attention of the king, the presidents, and the satraps. How can your actions be a witness of your faith in God?

2. God doesn't give us specific rules about when and how to pray; however, Daniel chose to pray on his knees, three times a day. What does Daniel's posture of prayer suggest about the nature of God and our relationship with God?

3. The Bible compares Satan to a roaring lion (1 Peter 5:8). God delivered Daniel from the lions. In what way has God delivered us from Satan?

59

Daniel Sees Heaven (Daniel 7)

Reviewing God's Word

Fill in the blanks.

1. Daniel saw a ____________________ as he lay in his bed.
2. The Ancient of ____________________ took His seat.
3. A stream of ______________ issued and came out from before Him.
4. A ________________________ thousands served God.
5. The court sat in judgment, and the __________________ were opened.
6. Behold, with the clouds of heaven there came one like a son of ______________________.
7. All ________________, nations, and languages should serve Him, the Son of Man.
8. His dominion is an ____________________ dominion, which shall not pass away.

Thinking about God's Word

1. Why did Daniel write down his visions?

2. Whom did Daniel see sitting upon the throne?

3. How did Daniel describe God?

4. Whom did Daniel see surrounding God?

5. What was the court of heaven doing?

6. Whom did Daniel say would serve the Son of Man (Jesus)?

7. What comfort did Daniel receive when his vision alarmed him?

Applying God's Word

1. How does Daniel's description of God help you understand what God is like?

2. What does it mean for us that Jesus, the Son of Man, was presented before the throne of the Father?

3. What does it mean to be one of "the saints of the Most High"?

60

A New Temple and a New Wall (The Books of Ezra; Nehemiah)

Reviewing God's Word

Circle Yes or No for each statement.

1. God commanded King Cyrus of Persia to build Him a house in Jerusalem.	YES	NO
2. King Cyrus himself provided the goods for the building of the temple.	YES	NO
3. The people of God resisted the command to return and rebuild.	YES	NO
4. The Jews and their neighbors freely offered aid.	YES	NO
5. The dedication of the temple involved a joyful Passover festival.	YES	NO
6. Nehemiah asked for permission to rebuild the wall of Jerusalem.	YES	NO
7. It took nearly a year to rebuild the city wall.	YES	NO
8. The nations around Judah were afraid when they saw the new wall.	YES	NO
9. The people celebrated the completion of the wall with music and sacrifices.	YES	NO

Thinking about God's Word

1. Why did King Cyrus tell the exiles to return to Jerusalem?

2. Who returned to Jerusalem?

3. How did the Israelites get the supplies they needed for the temple?

4. Why did Nehemiah ask to return to Jerusalem?

5. Why did Nehemiah tell the people they should rebuild the wall?

6. Why were the nations around Judah frightened?

Applying God's Word

1. King Cyrus probably didn't believe in the Lord, but God used him anyway to deliver the people of God from exile. What does this mean for how we view our rulers today?

2. Those "whose spirit God had stirred" worked to rebuild the temple. What does this tell us about why we do good works?

3. How might reading about the joy of the Israelites as they worshiped in the new temple affect our attitude toward worship?

61

Esther and the King

(Esther 1–2)

Reviewing God's Word

Draw lines to match each name to the correct description.

1. Ahasuerus	• Official in charge of the women
2. Esther	• Jew who saved the king's life
3. Mordecai	• High-ranking official to whom everyone had to bow
4. Vashti	• Young Jewish woman who won the king's favor and became queen
5. Haman	• King in Susa
6. Hegai	• Queen who refused to appear before the king at his feast

Thinking about God's Word

1. Why did King Ahasuerus want Queen Vashti to appear before him and his officials?

2. How were both the king and queen acting sinfully?

3. What did the king do with Queen Vashti?

4. Why is it important that both Mordecai and Esther were Jews?

5. What happened to Esther in the palace?

6. What did Mordecai do to earn himself a place in the king's record?

7. Why did Haman want to destroy the Jews?

Applying God's Word

1. The story of Esther is a beautiful example of how God directs events to accomplish His will. How does this account show God using even sinful actions to bring about His will?

2. How did Mordecai show godly care for Esther?

   Whom has God placed in your life to care for you?

3. Haman wanted to destroy all the Jews. Why could Mordecai and Esther be sure his plan wouldn't succeed?

62

God Saves His People (Esther 3–8)

Reviewing God's Word

Draw a line through the sentences that are not true.

1. King Ahasuerus came up with a plan to get rid of the Jews.
2. Mordecai asked Esther to go to the king and plead for the Jews.
3. Most people who went to the king uninvited were killed.
4. The king was angry that Esther came before his throne.
5. Esther told the king about Haman's wicked plot.
6. The king spared Haman because he was a powerful man.
7. Mordecai took over Haman's position in the king's court.

Thinking about God's Word

1. Why would it have taken great courage for Esther to approach the king?
2. How did Mordecai convince Esther to go to the king?
3. What was Esther's first request of the king?
4. What did Esther ask for from the king the second time he offered to grant any request?
5. Why would it have taken special courage for Esther to plead for her people at this feast?
6. How was Haman punished?
7. How did God bless Esther and Mordecai?
8. How did God deliver His people?

Applying God's Word

1. God placed Esther in the palace in order to deliver the Jews. In what way might God have placed you in your home or school or church "for such a time as this"?
2. Esther was afraid to approach the king because she knew she might be killed for coming before the throne uninvited. Why can you approach God's throne through prayer with joyful confidence?
3. Romans 8:34 says "Christ Jesus . . . is at the right hand of God . . . [and] is interceding for us." How is Esther's role in this account like Christ's role of intercessor?

63

Waiting for God's Messenger
(The Book of Malachi)

Reviewing God's Word

Draw lines to match each image to the idea it represents.

1. Incense	• Strong cleansing from sin
2. Refiner's fire	• Christ / warm light of the Gospel
3. Fuller's soap	• Joy and excitement over our salvation
4. Stubble	• Prayers
5. Sun of righteousness	• Protection and healing
6. Wings	• All the arrogant and evildoers
7. Leaping like calves	• Purifying nature of God's judgment

Thinking about God's Word

1. Where and when does Malachi say people will glorify God's name?

2. What does God mean when He compares Christ to a person who purifies metals?

3. How did the Lord show that He would remember those who believed in Him?

4. To what relationship does God compare His relationship with those who believe in Him?

5. How does God make it clear in Malachi that He does punish sin?

6. What does God promise to those who do fear His name?

Applying God's Word

1. What does this section from Malachi say about how God views sin?

2. Why can we face Judgment Day with all the carefree joy of a leaping calf?

3. After the end of the Old Testament, God's people had to wait and trust Him for over four hundred years for the coming of the Messiah. What coming are we waiting for, and how can we be sure it will happen?

64

The Birth of John Foretold (Luke 1)

Reviewing God's Word

Answer each question with names or words below. Some names will not be used.

1. Who was Zechariah's wife?
2. In what building was Zechariah burning incense?
3. What was the name of the angel God sent to Zechariah?
4. What was Zechariah's child to be named?
5. The child would have "the spirit and power" of what prophet?
6. Who was unable to speak until the child was born?
7. Name one other Bible woman who was blessed with a child in her old age.

Gabriel	Elijah	Palace
Temple	John	Zechariah
Elizabeth	Sarah	Joseph
Jesus	Michael	Mary

Thinking about God's Word

1. What great event was drawing near at the time of this lesson?
2. Which words tell that Zechariah and Elizabeth were God-fearing?
3. Why was Gabriel sent to tell Zechariah that his wife would give birth to a son?
4. Which words show that Gabriel came from God in answer to Zechariah's prayer?
5. Why did Zechariah ask, "How shall I know this?"

Applying God's Word

1. What is a messenger? How does John fit in this role?

   Can we be messengers for Jesus too? Explain.

2. The angel came to bring Zechariah good news. How does the angel's message relate to the greatest Good News of all?
3. Why is it sometimes hard for us to believe what God says? Can we trust that He will always keep His promises?

65

The Birth of Jesus Foretold (Luke 1; Matthew 1)

Reviewing God's Word

Draw lines to match the words to their meanings.

1. virgin	•title given to Jesus
2. favored	•to see; notice
3. Behold	•a promise of marriage
4. conceived	•woman who has not had sexual relations
5. betrothed	•greatly honored
6. Savior	•place in a woman's body where a baby develops
7. womb	•to become pregnant

Thinking about God's Word

1. Why was Mary afraid of the angel at first?

2. In which words did Mary say she did not understand how everything would happen that the angel had said?

3. With which words did Mary say that she would submit to God's plans for her?

4. How does the angel make clear that God, not Joseph, was to be the true Father of Jesus?

5. What did the angel tell Joseph that Jesus would do while on earth?

6. What was the Savior to be named, according to the angel's words?

Find three other names for Jesus from this lesson.

Applying God's Word

1. Which words of the Apostles' Creed are clearly referenced in Gabriel's message to Mary?

2. Which words of the lesson show that the Savior was to be true man, born of a woman?

3. Why was it necessary for the world's Savior to be a human?

66

The Birth of John
(Luke 1)

Reviewing God's Word

Underline the word or phrase that answers each question.

1. On which day after the baby was born was he circumcised? (Eighth—Fifth—Seventh—First)
2. What did the neighbors want to name the baby? (John—Joseph—David—Zechariah)
3. What did the Elizabeth insist that the baby should be named? (Zechariah—John—Jesus—David)
4. For whom was this child to prepare the way? (Jesus—Moses—His servant David—John)
5. Who asked for a writing tablet? (Elizabeth—The relatives—Zechariah—The angel)
6. Where was John until the day he appeared to Israel? (In the wilderness—In his father's house—In the temple—In prayer)

Thinking about God's Word

1. How did God's promise to Zechariah and Elizabeth come true?

2. Why did Elizabeth's neighbors and relatives question whether the child should be named John?

3. In the naming of their son, how did the parents show that they had learned to obey and trust God without question?

4. How did Zechariah settle the matter of naming the child?

   After that, how were the angel's words fulfilled?

5. How did Zechariah use his loosed tongue, which once had spoken words of doubt at God's promise?

6. What did Zechariah prophesy about his son?

Applying God's Word

1. Which words, prophesied by Zechariah, refer to the work of Jesus, our Savior?

2. When our sinful doubt and personal understanding seems to advise us to follow the plans of our heart, to whom should we be really listening?

   Why?

3. How can you show your thankfulness to God for having kept His promises?

67

The Birth of Jesus
(Luke 2)

Reviewing God's Word

Underline the word that makes each sentence true.

1. (Caesar Augustus—Quirinius—Julius) was the governor of Syria when Jesus was born.
2. Everyone had to go to (Rome—his own town—Bethlehem) to be registered.
3. Mary and Joseph traveled to Bethlehem from the city of (Syria—Jerusalem—Nazareth).
4. Mary and Joseph belonged to the line of (Joseph—David—Mary).
5. (Jerusalem—Nazareth—Bethlehem) was the city of David.
6. When the angel appeared, the shepherds in the field were (excited—terrified—curious).
7. Mary treasured up all these things and (buried—gave thanks—pondered) them in her heart.
8. (David—Joseph—God) was the true Father of the Child Jesus.

Thinking about God's Word

1. How did God use Caesar Augustus to bring Mary and Joseph to the place where Jesus was to be born?
2. Which simple words tell how the Savior of the world was born at Bethlehem?
3. What kind of birth announcement did God send when Jesus was born?
4. How do you know the shepherds believed the angels?
5. Which words show that Mary, the mother of Jesus, remembered all these events?
6. What difference would it make to us if Jesus had not been born?
7. Who gave the Christ Child to us as a gift of love? Find the answer in John 3:16.

Applying God's Word

1. Of what should the giving of presents at Christmas remind Christians?
2. Why is the birth of Jesus such a significant event?
3. Who told you the good news of how Jesus was born for you?

   How can you show your appreciation for having been told these wonderful things?
4. How will Jesus' second coming be similar to and different from His first entrance into the world?

68

The Visit of the Wise Men (Matthew 2)

Reviewing God's Word

Answer each question with words or phrases from below. Some words will not be used.

1. From where did the Wise Men originally come?
2. At which city did they stop for information?
3. What did the Wise Men call Jesus?
4. Who was troubled about the Wise Men's question?
5. What was the age of the oldest boys that Herod killed?
6. Where was Joseph to flee with Mary and Jesus?
7. To what city in Israel did Joseph bring his family after trouble passed?

Two	The East	Persia
Four	Egypt	King of the Jews
Jerusalem	Herod	Messiah
Nazareth	Bethlehem	Scribes

Thinking about God's Word

1. Why did the Wise Men need a star to guide them from their land to the Holy Land?
2. How did the chief priests and scribes of Jesus' time discover where the Savior was to be born? See Micah 5:2.
3. Why was Herod disturbed at the words of the Wise Men?

   What was the lie Herod told regarding what he would do after Jesus was found?
4. Why did Herod ask the Wise Men to let him know where Jesus was to be found?

   Why did God warn the Wise Men not to tell Herod where Jesus was?
5. How did the Wise Men show they believed Jesus is God?
6. Jeremiah prophesied the "Slaughter of the Innocents" (see Jeremiah 31:15), which took place at this time. In what respect were the young boys in Bethlehem innocent?
7. Why are God's children happy to know that the angels are always near them?

   How did God use angels in this story?

Applying God's Word

1. What did Herod not understand about Jesus' kingship? See Jesus' words to Pilate in John 18:33–37.
2. The Wise Men brought Jesus gifts with a lot of earthly value. As we gather in church to worship Jesus, what can we remember about everything we are and possess?
3. How did God defend Jesus against all danger and guard and protect Him from all evil when He was a baby?

   How does God do the same for you daily?

69

The Boy Jesus in the Temple (Luke 2)

Reviewing God's Word

Draw a line through the sentences that are not true.

1. Each year, Jesus' parents traveled back to Bethlehem for the Feast of the Passover.
2. Even though Jesus wasn't with them, His parents left with their group to go home at the end of the feast.
3. At the time of this story, Jesus was twelve years old.
4. Mary and Joseph assumed that Jesus would start walking home eventually.
5. Jesus' parents returned to Jerusalem because they could not find Him in the group.
6. After three hours of searching, they finally found Him at the temple.
7. Mary was glad that Jesus was talking to teachers in the temple.
8. The teachers were amazed by the way Jesus interacted with them—questioning, listening, and understanding.
9. After His mother greeted Him, Jesus said, "I should have told you that I wanted to stay here."
10. Jesus obeyed His parents by leaving the temple with them to return to Nazareth.

Thinking about God's Word

1. Which words tell that Jesus' parents were obeying a requirement that God had put in place for the Israelites? Hint: see Deuteronomy 16:6.

2. Why did Jesus study Scripture even though "all the treasures of wisdom and knowledge" (Colossians 2:3) are to be found in Him?

3. Which words tell that Mary and Joseph were very worried over the thought of losing Jesus?

4. How did Jesus reply to His mother when she shared about her concern about Him?

   What did Jesus mean when He said this?

5. In what other recent story did Luke record that Mary treasured in her heart the events of Jesus' life?

Applying God's Word

1. What details of this account show Jesus to be true God? What details of this account show Jesus to be truly human?

2. How have you come to learn and know Scripture? Name people and things that have helped your spiritual growth.

3. Two commandments of God were clearly obeyed by Jesus in this lesson. What are they? How did Jesus obey them? How can we follow God's laws in these ways?

70

John Baptizes Jesus
(Matthew 3; John 1)

Reviewing God's Word

Underline the word or phrase that answers each question.

1. What was the theme of the message John preached? (Repentance—Rejoicing—Waiting—Forgiveness)
2. John baptized with water; what did he say Jesus would baptize with? (Water—God—Incense—Holy Spirit)
3. Whom did John feel unworthy to baptize? (Citizens of Jerusalem—Jesus—A Pharisee—Mary)
4. Which Old Testament prophet did John quote? (Isaiah—Malachi—Jeremiah—Ezekiel)
5. Read 1 Peter 3:18–21. Our Baptism is (a removal of dirt—a symbol of the start of our Christian life—salvation through Christ's death and resurrection—a promise of eternal life someday).

Thinking about God's Word

1. In his preaching, John said that it was time to repent. Why?
2. Some priests and Levites asked John who he was, and John clarified that he was neither Elijah nor Christ. How did he describe himself?
3. Why was John angry when the Pharisees and Sadducees came to him to be baptized?
4. How can you tell that John recognized Jesus as the Christ?
5. What reason did Jesus give John for being baptized by him?
6. How did God show Jesus as the Savior whom He had promised to send?
7. How was each person of the Trinity revealed at this Baptism?

Applying God's Word

1. Why did Jesus not need to be baptized as a sign of repentance?

   Why, then, was He baptized?
2. Three years later, after Jesus rose from the dead, He instructed His disciples to baptize "all nations" (Matthew 28:19). Does this command include babies too? Explain.
3. When we were baptized, the sign of the cross was made on our forehead and over our heart. What does this mean? Why is this sign a continual reminder of our Baptism?

71

The Temptation of Jesus (Matthew 4)

Reviewing God's Word

Fill in the blanks, using the words below. Some words will not be used.

1. Jesus was led into the wilderness by the ____________.
2. He fasted ________________ days and nights.
3. The devil asked Jesus to turn ____________ to bread.
4. Jesus said, "You shall not put the ________________ to the test."
5. The devil showed Jesus all the ________________ of the world.
6. The devil asked Jesus to fall down and ____________ him.
7. Jesus said, "Be gone, ________________."
8. Three times Jesus said, "It is ________________."
9. Angels came and ____________________ to Jesus.

written	ministered	forty
kingdoms	Spirit	gold
Satan	stones	protected
worship	Lord your God	twenty-five

Thinking about God's Word

1. Into whose power had man fallen when Adam sinned?

   Why had Jesus come into the world?

2. With what words did the devil first try to plant the seed of doubt into Jesus, as he once had done to Adam and Eve?

3. According to Jesus' words, by what shall man really live?

4. When Satan tempted Jesus the second time, how did he try to twist God's Word to lead Jesus into sin?

   How did Satan twist God's Word in the Garden of Eden?

5. In the third temptation, how did the devil use humankind's love for honor and possessions to try to lead Jesus into sin?

   How had he used the same kind of temptation against Adam and Eve?

6. Satan tried to tempt Jesus my misquoting God's Word. How did Jesus respond?

7. What was Jesus' final answer to the devil's temptations?

8. Why did Satan want to keep Jesus from doing His work?

   How did the devil plan to spoil what Jesus had come to do?

Applying God's Word

1. What was the difference in outcome between Satan's attempt to lead Adam into sin and his attempt to lead Jesus into sin?

2. This account shows how Jesus obeyed God's Law in our place. Explain.

3. In facing and resisting temptation, Jesus pointed us to the means through which the Holy Spirit strengthens us to resist temptations. What is that means?

72

Jesus Calls Disciples (John 1; Luke 5)

Reviewing God's Word

Draw lines to match each name to the actions that fit the person.

1. Jesus	• was introduced to Jesus by Philip.
2. Nathanael	• heard John speaking of Jesus.
3. Andrew	• was from Bethsaida.
4. Levi	• spoke of "catching men."
5. Simon	• said, "Behold, the Lamb of God!"
6. Philip	• was a tax collector.
7. John the Baptist	• wrote about Jesus before His coming.
8. Moses	• was given the name "Cephas" by Jesus.

Thinking about God's Word

1. Why do you think the first thing Andrew told his brother Simon was "We have found the Messiah"?

2. How do you think Philip felt when Jesus turned to him and said, "Follow Me"?

3. How do you know that people in this story were eager to hear God's Word?

   What do you think Jesus talked about to the people?

4. Why did Simon not seem to think they should try fishing again?

   What was it that made him willing to let down the net, nevertheless?

5. How did Peter show that he knew he had seen a miracle?

6. After the large number of fish was caught, why might Jesus have told Simon not to be afraid?

7. How did the disciples show that they believed and trusted in Jesus?

Applying God's Word

1. Even though the disciples had not known Jesus for very long at the time He called them, what knowledge did they have of Him that allowed them to trust Him and follow?

   Why do we have peace by knowing that Jesus is the Savior?

2. Simon Peter's exclamation of doubt—"Master, we toiled all night and took nothing!"—sounds like something we would say. Explain.

3. What does the amount of fish in the catch show about the growth expected in God's kingdom?

73

Jesus Changes Water to Wine (John 2)

Reviewing God's Word

Fill in the blanks, using the words below. Some words will not be used.

1. There was a wedding in the city of ________________.
2. Mary, Jesus, and His ________________ were among some of the guests.
3. The people ran out of ________________.
4. Jesus said, "My ________________ has not yet come."
5. Mary told the ________________ to do whatever Jesus might command.
6. By His power, Jesus turned the ____________ into good wine.
7. Jesus' ______________ was revealed during this miracle.

servants	day	guests
Nazareth	wine	water
hour	Cana	father
forgiveness	glory	disciples

Thinking about God's Word

1. Why was it not hard for Jesus' followers to believe that He was a true man?

2. Who went to Jesus for help when the wine had run out?

   Why should we go to Jesus in prayer when we need help?

3. Why might Jesus have told His mother "My hour has not yet come"?

4. How did Jesus show Himself to be true God before the people at Cana?

5. What did Jesus use to turn water into wine?

6. To whom was some water taken after it had been changed to wine?

7. Which words tell how the disciples reacted after Jesus performed this miracle?

Applying God's Word

1. Tell how this account shows Jesus as both true man and true God.

2. Mary had great faith in Jesus' power, as seen in her statement "Do whatever He tells you." Read Hebrews 11:1 and explain what faith means.

3. What does this account indicate about the scope of human problems about which Jesus is concerned?

74

Jesus Clears the Temple (John 2)

Reviewing God's Word

Circle Yes or No for each statement.

1. The Jews in the temple welcomed Jesus when He arrived for the Passover.	YES	NO
2. Jesus made a whip to drive the sellers out of the area.	YES	NO
3. God's house had been turned into a "house of trade."	YES	NO
4. Jesus told the people they had to leave as soon as they finished their sales.	YES	NO
5. Jesus was angry because the Jews in the temple were disrespecting His Father's house.	YES	NO
6. The temple that Jesus promised to raise in three days would be made of stone.	YES	NO

Thinking about God's Word

1. Why would Jesus, who was called the Prince of Peace by the prophet Isaiah (9:6), make a whip to drive people out of the temple?

2. Selling livestock is not a sinful occupation. What reason did Jesus give the sellers and traders as to His just anger?

3. The Jews asked, "What sign do You show us for doing these things?" What does this tell about their opinion of Jesus and His actions?

4. Why might Jesus have spoken about His coming resurrection in order to answer the Jews?

5. Which parts of this story indicate that the disciples paid close attention to the words of the prophets and their Teacher, Jesus?

Applying God's Word

1. The sinfulness of God's people was very visible in the temple—they were buying and selling in a place that God had declared holy and set aside for worship. They stopped caring about God's order and commands. In what ways is our body similar to the temple in this story?

2. When the Jews asked Jesus for a sign in order to understand His actions, it was almost as if they were saying, "Who do you think You are?" Later in Jesus' ministry, He asked Simon Peter, "Who do people say that the Son of Man is?" (Matthew 16:13). Why is it important that we know exactly who Jesus is?

3. After clearing out the temple, Jesus took the opportunity to address the Jews' doubts about Him by pointing to His resurrection. The Jews could not make sense of His prophesy, but the disciples committed these words to heart. If we interact with nonbelievers, what can we learn from Jesus' eagerness to point to His new life?

75

Jesus Teaches Nicodemus (John 3)

Reviewing God's Word

Fill in the blanks, using the words of Jesus below. Some words may be used more than once or not at all.

1. "Unless one is born of ________________ and the Spirit, he cannot enter the kingdom of God."
2. "We speak of what we ___________________________."
3. "As Moses ________________ up the serpent in the wilderness, so must the Son of Man be ___________ up."
4. "Whoever ________________ in Him should not perish but have eternal life."
5. "For God did not send His Son into the world to ________________ the world."
6. "The ________________ has come into the world, and people loved the darkness."
7. "Whoever does what is true comes to the light, so that it may be clearly seen that his ______________ have been carried out in God."

believes	fail	perish
light	know	water
works	lifted	actions
strength	condemn	express

Thinking about God's Word

1. Why did Nicodemus decide to visit Jesus at night?

2. With which words does Nicodemus show he recognizes that God's power is at work in Jesus?

3. What Means of Grace is Jesus referring to when He tells Nicodemus that one must be "born of water and the Spirit" to enter the kingdom of God?

4. The story of Moses raising up the image of a bronze snake on a pole in order to heal God's dying people is found in Numbers 21:4–9. Tell about the connection between this story and Jesus' crucifixion.

5. What (or who) is "the light" that Jesus speaks of? Hint: see John 8:12.

   What does He mean by "the darkness"?

6. At the end of this story, by whom does Jesus say that our works have been carried out?

Applying God's Word

1. Nicodemus confesses his understanding that someone can do the great miracles Jesus had performed only if "God is with him." Little did he know how much truth was in this insight! How would you explain to Nicodemus that God was more than just "with" Jesus?

2. What does Jesus' statement "the light has come into the world, and the people loved the darkness rather than the light" say about sinful people's reaction to God's Son walking among them? See also John 1:9–11.

3. If our good works are carried out in God, should we be prideful when we serve others? Explain.

76

Jesus and the Samaritan Woman

(John 4)

Reviewing God's Word

Draw a line through the sentences that are not true.

1. Jesus' disciples told Him about Jacob's well near Samaria, and they set out to sample the water.
2. While He was waiting at the well for His disciples to return from the city, Jesus met a woman.
3. It was not uncommon for a Jewish man and a Samaritan woman to have a conversation in public.
4. Jesus told the woman that He could give her living water that quenches thirst forever.
5. The Samaritan woman told Jesus that she had no husband to bring to Him.
6. Once Jesus revealed He knew the woman's past, she exclaimed "Messiah!"
7. Samaritans from the town believed in Jesus both because of the woman's testimony and Jesus' teaching.

Thinking about God's Word

1. If Jewish people were not supposed to interact with Samaritans, why might Jesus have talked to the woman at the well?
2. The woman did not immediately understand that she was talking to the Messiah. Why then is it reasonable that she was confused by a description of "living water"?
3. Which words of Jesus tell what happens to those who are given this special water?
4. When the woman eagerly asks for the water that Jesus speaks about, how does He respond?
5. From Scripture, it is clear that God is omnipotent (all powerful), omniscient (all knowing), and omnipresent (all present). Which of these attributes is made obvious during Jesus' interaction with the woman?
6. How does Jesus reveal His messianic identity to the woman?

Applying God's Word

1. Against cultural norms, Jesus began talking to the Samaritan woman because she was dear to His Father in heaven. What can this teach us as we look for opportunities to share the Good News?
2. Which Sacrament involves being washed with God's life-giving water? Which person of the Holy Trinity is poured out on God's children at that time?
3. One of three ways that God uses His Law is to lead us to recognize our sin. In which part of this story is Jesus using the Law in this way?

77

Jesus Rejected at Nazareth (Luke 4)

Reviewing God's Word

Circle Yes or No for each statement.

1. Jesus went to the synagogue in Nazareth because it was the Sabbath day.	YES	NO
2. All in the synagogue were impressed that Jesus recited Isaiah's words from memory.	YES	NO
3. Jesus said to the people, "This Scripture is soon to be fulfilled before you."	YES	NO
4. The people remembered Jesus only as Joseph's son, and they were amazed by His words.	YES	NO
5. According to Jesus, "Only a prophet who speaks in his hometown is acceptable."	YES	NO
6. When Jesus spoke of Elijah and Elisha's time, he mentioned only Gentile believers.	YES	NO
7. In this story, God protected His Son from death before it was His time.	YES	NO

Thinking about God's Word

1. Why do you think Luke makes a point of mentioning that Nazareth was where Jesus "had been brought up"?

2. Considering that Jesus was fully God as well as man, what seems unusual about the fact that He read from the scroll of the prophet Isaiah?

3. According to Jesus, who is "He" and who is "Me" in the prophetic phrase "He has sent Me to proclaim liberty"?

4. Which words tell that Jesus had a captive audience when He began preaching?

5. Jesus' message to the people at the synagogue that day was that God does not withhold mercy from those who are Gentiles, or non-Jewish. What two Old Testament examples did He share to show this truth?

6. When Jesus had finished teaching, the people were angry and attempted to kill Him by throwing Him off a cliff. How did He escape this danger?

Applying God's Word

1. Why did the people in the synagogue become "filled with wrath" after Jesus preached?

2. In what way is Jesus' passing through the people's midst similar to the event when an angel appeared to Joseph, telling him to flee with Mary and Jesus to Egypt?

3. Just as it is true that a prophet is not accepted in his hometown, it can also be difficult to confess our faith to people we know really well and who may have known us throughout our childhood. "What will they think of me if I tell about the truth?" How do Jesus' words in Matthew 10:22 respond to this fear?

78

Jesus Heals a Paralyzed Man (Mark 2)

Reviewing God's Word

Underline the word or phrase that makes each sentence true.

1. Jesus was inside a (house—synagogue—temple) when the paralyzed man was brought to Him.
2. The first thing Jesus did for the man was to (ask his name—heal his sickness—forgive his sins).
3. (Jesus—The sick man—The scribes) said, "Who can forgive sins but God alone?"
4. Jesus called Himself (the Messiah—the Son of Man—the Savior) in this lesson.
5. The teachers spoke evil things of Jesus (in their hearts—so that all could hear—in a low voice).
6. Jesus told the sick man to pick up his (belongings—bed—scroll) and go home.
7. The people who saw this miracle (laughed at the scribes—told Jesus to leave their country—glorified God).

Thinking about God's Word

1. Why did the four men bring their sick friend to Jesus?
2. How did these men show their faith in Jesus' power to help?
3. Which words of Jesus tell what the man actually needed more than the healing of his body?
4. Why did the scribes think that Jesus had mocked God?
5. Answer the question that Jesus posed to the scribes: "Which is easier, to say to the paralytic, 'Your sins are forgiven,' or to say, 'Rise, take up your bed and walk'?
6. What reason did Jesus give for deciding to physically heal the man of his paralysis?

Applying God's Word

1. The friends of the paralyzed man went to great lengths to be in Jesus' presence in order that He might richly bless their friend with healing. Today, Jesus gives us good gifts of healing as we gather for worship in God's house. Give an example of a time when your attitude was not like that of the man's friends.
2. Jesus blessed the paralyzed man with two incredible acts of healing, one of body and one of spirit. Which of these do you think is more important? Why?
3. What connections can you make between this man's friends taking Him to Jesus and parents bringing their newborn child to the waters of Baptism?

79

The Sermon on the Mount (Matthew 5–7)

Reviewing God's Word

Fill in the blanks, using the words below. Some words will not be used.

1. Blessed are those who ________________, for they shall be comforted.
2. Blessed are the pure in heart, for they shall __________ God.
3. Rejoice, for your __________ is great in __________.
4. Love your ________________ and pray for those who persecute you.
5. Your Father knows what you need before you __________ Him.
6. Give us this day our daily bread, and forgive us our ________________.
7. Lead us not into temptation, but deliver us from ________________.
8. He was ____________ them as one who had authority.

fight	know	see	stupidity
enemies	debts	heaven	teaching
Christ	reward	ask	worshiping
strength	battles	call	rest
fail	mourn	evil	flee

Thinking about God's Word

1. The pattern of the first part of Jesus' sermon involves Him listing the blessings that are given to those who recognize their sin and turn to Him in faith. Name some of the blessings that are given to God's people.

2. Where does "the light" come from that Jesus speaks of when He says His followers "are the light of the world?"

3. Which words of Jesus tell that God loves and provides for believers and unbelievers alike?

4. What might Jesus mean by instructing the people to not pray "empty phrases as the Gentiles do"? Didn't He come to earth to bring salvation for Jews and Gentiles?

5. Everyone who hears Jesus' words but "does not do them" will be like whom?

Applying God's Word

1. When Jesus describes people as "poor in spirit" and "those who mourn," He is not talking about any physical problems or sadness but rather about our spiritual poverty and mourning that comes about as a result of sin. Does this mean He might forget about your physical needs?

2. As you reflect on Jesus' teaching that our light shines so that others "see [our] good works and give glory to [our] Father who is in heaven," explain why the statement "I won some souls today" is incorrect.

3. Edward Mote wrote the line "My hope is built on nothing less Than Jesus' blood and righteousness" as the opening to a well-known hymn. Does this describe the man who built his house on the rock or the man who chose to build on the sand? Why?

80

Jesus Calms a Storm
(Mark 4)

Reviewing God's Word

For the following statements in Mark's Gospel, circle T for true and F for false.

1. "Jesus was tired and fell asleep by the sea."	T	F
2. "Jesus said to His disciples, 'Let us go across to the other side'."	T	F
3. "And no other boats were with Him."	T	F
4. "A great windstorm arose."	T	F
5. "The disciples wondered if Jesus would wake up."	T	F
6. "Do You not care that we are perishing?"	T	F
7. "Has your faith not been strengthened?"	T	F

Thinking about God's Word

1. How can it be shown from this lesson that Jesus was true man?

2. Why did the disciples awaken Jesus?

3. With what words did Jesus calm the storm?

4. Why did the wind and sea obey Jesus?

5. Show from this lesson that Jesus was true God and true man.

6. What words of the disciples suggest they may have doubted Jesus, even while they asked Him for help?

7. Why might Jesus have responded to their fear by saying "Have you still no faith"?

6. Who permitted this great storm to come up?

Why does God let trials and temptations come to His children?

Applying God's Word

1. Psalm 121:4 says God "will neither slumber nor sleep." What does this mean for you?

2. John 1:3 says, "All things were made through Him, and without Him was not any thing made that was made." Who is "Him" in this verse? How does this verse help us understand Jesus' command over the storm?

3. Why do you think the disciples ask one another "who then is this?" with regard to Jesus? Don't they know the identity of Him who called on them to follow?

81

Jesus Heals Jairus's Daughter (Mark 5)

Reviewing God's Word

Underline the word or phrase that answers each question.

1. What was soon to happen to Jairus's young daughter? She would (become sick—die—prophesy—possess demons).
2. How did Jairus suggest Jesus could help his daughter? (Lay His hands on her—Bring living water to her—Cast the demon out of her—Talk to her)
3. What did the sick woman in the crowd do in order to be healed? (Called out to Jesus—Stopped Jesus' disciples—Touched Jesus' garment—Spoke to Jairus)
4. What did Jesus call death in this lesson? (Rest—Sleep—The end of everything—Heaven)
5. How did the people in Jairus's house show unbelief in Jesus? (They cast Him out—They laughed at Him—They left the room—They closed their ears)
6. How old was Jairus's sick daughter? (30—12—21—5—6)
7. What was Jesus' first instruction to those in the room who witnessed the miracle? (Tell no one—Spread the news—Feed the girl—Let the girl rest)

Thinking about God's Word

1. How did Jairus show his faith in Jesus?
2. In what way was the sick woman's understanding of Jesus' ability to heal similar to that of Jairus?
3. After the woman had already felt her healing take place, how did Jesus explain the way she had been cured?
4. When people from Jairus's house brought news of His daughter's death, what did they suggest Jesus should do?
5. What did Jesus mean when He said, "The child is not dead but sleeping"?
6. How did Jesus show the people of Jairus's household that His power over death meant resurrection was possible?
7. At what other time did Jesus prove that He had the ultimate victory over the grave?

Applying God's Word

1. Even though Jairus's daughter was near death, Jairus didn't turn to despair. What did he do instead? How should we react when faced with a scary situation?
2. Jesus told the sick woman that her faith had made her well. Who gave her that faith?
3. Because of Jesus, the death of Jairus's daughter was really just a short sleep that had a joyful ending. Why does death mean the same thing for you too?

82

Jesus Feeds Five Thousand (John 6)

Reviewing God's Word

Draw a line through the sentences that are not true.

1. A few people followed Jesus across the Sea of Galilee, and more joined when they heard about a meal.
2. At the time of this story, the Feast of the Passover was about to take place.
3. Jesus asked Philip where they should buy bread to feed the crowd as a way to test him.
4. In response, Philip pointed out a young boy who already had loaves of bread and fish.
5. Jesus said, "Have the people gather around me for the blessing."
6. All the people in the crowd were able to eat until they were full.
7. When the crowd saw this sign, some inwardly questioned Jesus' authority.

Thinking about God's Word

1. Why did a large crowd follow Jesus when He crossed the sea and went up on a mountain?
2. What did Philip's answer show that he thought was of first importance in getting food for hungry people?
3. Why do you think Jesus tested Philip with a question about how to provide for Jesus' followers?
4. What made Andrew's observation of the small boy seem at first like an impossible solution?
5. What did Jesus do before He distributed the bread to the crowd?
6. In which prayer do we say, "Give us this day our daily bread"?

   Why do we ask for it, even when we know we'll get it?

Applying God's Word

1. Jesus' miracles led the people to see Jesus as a great prophet. But, Jesus is more than a prophet. Explain.
2. Jesus could have simply taken away the people's hunger. Instead, He satisfied their hunger by multiplying a meager lunch of bread and fish. In another meal, the Lord's Supper, Jesus also provides for His disciples (then and now). What do they receive with the bread and wine?

   What benefits are received?
3. After He fed the crowd and commanded the gathering of leftovers, Jesus withdrew, because He knew the people would want to "take Him by force to make Him king." Why would Jesus not have wanted this to happen?

83

Jesus Walks on Water
(Matthew 14)

Reviewing God's Word

Answer each question with a word or phrase from below. Not all words will be used.

1. Whom did Jesus send away?
2. What was Jesus doing while He was on the mountain alone?
3. During which watch did Jesus come to His disciples?
4. What did the disciples think Jesus was when they saw Him?
5. With which word did Jesus tell Peter to walk out to Him?
6. What describes Peter's feelings when he saw the wind?
7. With what name did the disciples acknowledge Jesus' identity?

crowd	afraid	come	Son of God
fourth	ghost	praying	follow
Peter	planning	last	Christ

Thinking about God's Word

1. Why were the disciples not waiting for Jesus when He came down the mountain from praying?
2. How did the disciples show that they didn't believe that it was Jesus when they saw Him coming toward them?
3. What did Jesus say to them?

   How did those words show why He had come to them?
4. Why could Jesus walk on water?

   Why could Peter walk on water?
5. What did Peter cry out when he began to sink?
6. Which words of Jesus tell why Peter began to sink?

   How did Jesus show Peter that He was the merciful Son of God?
7. What two things happened when Jesus climbed into the boat?

Applying God's Word

1. Jesus spoke to His disciples in their fear, saying, "Take heart; it is I. Do not be afraid." How do these words of Jesus apply also to us?
2. As soon as Peter began to look at the scary environment around him, he began to sink. In what way are we like Peter?
3. This was not the first time the disciples had witnessed Jesus' power over the created elements, but their responses to Jesus' miracle of calming the wind was drastically different in this story. Compare their reactions.

84

Jesus Is Anointed
(Luke 7)

Reviewing God's Word

Circle Yes or No for each statement.

1. Jesus was walking by a Pharisee's house, and He asked to eat with him.	YES	NO
2. The sinful woman began weeping as she stood in Jesus' presence.	YES	NO
3. The Pharisee took pity on the woman because of her repentant cries.	YES	NO
4. Jesus called the Pharisee by his name.	YES	NO
5. In Jesus' analogy with the debtors, the sinful woman at His feet is represented by the debtor who owed the most to the moneylender.	YES	NO
6. The Pharisee objected to Jesus' accusations regarding his lack of hospitality.	YES	NO
7. Jesus said, "He who is forgiven little, loves little."	YES	NO

Thinking about God's Word

1. In previous stories, the Pharisees were intrigued by Jesus, but they were often provoked to anger by His teachings and the way He used His authority. Name one action of Simon the Pharisee that makes him similar to others in his group.

2. The woman did not say a word during this event. In what four ways did she show that she was deeply grieved by her sin?

3. Which part of this story reveals Jesus' omniscience?

4. In Jesus' story about the moneylenders, what does the debt stand for? Think about the point that Jesus made.

5. According to Jesus' final words to the woman, why was she now clean to stand in His presence?

Applying God's Word

1. Recall the Beatitudes that Jesus taught during His sermon on the mount. Which of these promises especially speak to the woman who came to Jesus? Why?

2. In Mark 2:17, Jesus said, "I came not to call the righteous, but sinners." Did the Pharisee need to hear these words? Do you?

3. What would you say to a person who shares a desire to be forgiven but is worried that he or she has done too much wrong for Jesus to love him or her?

85

Peter's Confession and Jesus' Transfiguration (Matthew 16; Mark 9)

Reviewing God's Word

Fill in the blanks, using the words below. Some words will not be used.

Jesus asked His disciples who ________________ thought the Son of Man was. "Some say John the Baptist, others say ________________, and others Jeremiah or one of the ________________," they replied. Jesus said to them, "Who do ____________ say that I am?" ____________________ told Jesus their belief that He is the ____________. Jesus said that "flesh and blood" had not ____________ that truth to him, but His Father in heaven. This knowledge has power over ____________.

war	death	Elijah	flesh
people	Simon Peter	scribes	Christ
cripples	John	revealed	you
prophets	transfigured	hell	Pharisees

Fill in the blanks with words from below.

Jesus took ____________, ____________, and John up a mountain. He was ______________ before them. Two men, ____________ and ______________, appeared with Jesus. Peter offered to build ____________ for the three men. A voice came from a ____________, saying Jesus is God's ______________. ____________ told the disciples not to tell what they had seen.

Moses	Jesus	Elijah	covered
two	six	Son	pillar
Peter	John	James	choice
cloud	transfigured	tents	fires

Thinking about God's Word

1. Which words show that the people on earth during Jesus' time had different ideas about who the Son of Man was?

2. According to Jesus, who was helping Peter answer Jesus' question about His identity?

3. When Jesus says "you," He is talking about all the disciples —those present with Him then and those throughout the world now. To what will Jesus' disciples be given the keys?

4. What did Jesus look like in His transfiguration?

5. What did Peter want to do for Jesus? Why?

6. Why were the disciples terrified?

7. What did the voice from the cloud say? Who was speaking?

8. When would the disciples be able to tell people what they had seen on the mountain?

Applying God's Word

1. In the story of Jesus' transfiguration, the disciples heard God the Father's message that Jesus is His Son. Up until that time, they had not seen Jesus appear to them in His glory. Why, then, is Peter's confession (in the first story) so remarkable? How is our confession about Jesus like Peter's?

2. Jesus said, "On this rock I will build My Church." The "rock" He is talking about is the confession that Jesus is the Christ, the Son of God. What is wrong with the belief that all different religions can bring you into God's kingdom?

3. Tell the meaning of the words spoken from the bright cloud for the disciples and for you.

86

Jesus Sends the Seventy-Two (Luke 10)

Reviewing God's Word

Underline the word that makes each sentence true.

1. The Lord appointed (12—72—45) men to go ahead of Him to preach about the kingdom of God.
2. Before the men left, Jesus told them that "the (land—water—harvest) is plentiful, but the laborers are few."
3. "I am sending you out as lambs in the midst of (war—wolves—confusion).
4. "Say to them, 'The (kingdom—love—Law) of God has come near to you.'"
5. "The one who hears you (rejects—calls—hears) Me."
6. "I saw (God—rulers—Satan) fall like lightning from heaven."
7. "Rejoice that your (actions—names—hearts) are written in heaven."

Thinking about God's Word

1. Where did Jesus send the seventy-two?

2. The "harvest" that Jesus referred to was the task of calling human souls into His kingdom. The "laborers" are people who work to tell others about the kingdom of God. Which category do the seventy-two fall under—souls in need of salvation or laborers who preach God's word?

3. What three items are the men not supposed to bring during their travels?

4. How will the men be provided with food and drink along the way?

5. What are the men supposed to do if a town does not receive them?

6. Jesus says that "the one who rejects Me rejects Him who sent Me." Rewrite this sentence in your own words.

7. When the seventy-two return from their mission, they are excited about Jesus' power over demons. Jesus says there is a better reason to be joyful. Why should the men have rejoiced?

Applying God's Word

1. The "laborers" that God sends out today are His people who have come to faith in Jesus by God's grace and who now tell others about the Gospel. Who are some people in your life who told you about the way to heaven?

2. Jesus tells the men to bring few belongings on their journey, because they will be provided for by people they meet along the way. In this, Jesus emphasized being content with their living situation so they could focus on teaching about God's kingdom. According to these instructions, what should be our top focus in life?

3. If we have a chance to tell someone what Jesus has done for him or her, should we expect that person to become a Christian? Explain. Hint: does Jesus say that all people will receive Him?

87

The Good Samaritan (Luke 10)

Reviewing God's Word

For the following statements, circle T for true and F for false.

1. The lawyer's question about how to inherit eternal life was to test Jesus.	T	F
2. After the lawyer summarized the Law, Jesus said, "And you can never fulfill this to live."	T	F
3. While going to Jerusalem, a man fell into the hands of robbers.	T	F
4. The man called out for help, but no one came to him.	T	F
5. A priest tended to the man's wounds.	T	F
6. A Samaritan had compassion on the man.	T	F
7. The wounded man was the Good Samaritan.	T	F
8. A neighbor to others is one who shows mercy.	T	F

Thinking about God's Word

1. What two questions did the lawyer, the expert in the law, wish to have answered?

2. How did Jesus respond to the lawyer's first question?

3. According to Jesus, did the lawyer interpret the Law correctly? Explain.

4. Which words tell that the wounded man's condition was severe?

5. How did the priest and the Levite react when they saw the injured man?

6. By using a parable, what lesson did Jesus teach the lawyer?

7. In what ways was the Samaritan a neighbor, or one who showed mercy, to the wounded man?

8. What did Jesus ask the lawyer, the expert in the law, at the end of His parable?

Applying God's Word

1. In response to the lawyer's summary of the Law (what God asks of us), Jesus told him that if he did this, he would live. This message is not very comforting to sinners like us. Why?

2. God instructs all of His people to show mercy to those around them; as a result, believers and unbelievers alike become our neighbors. List some specific tasks that involve showing compassion to other people.

3. How did Jesus prove Himself to be a good neighbor to us?

88

Jesus Heals a Blind Man (John 9)

Reviewing God's Word

Draw lines to match each name with the action that fits the person or place.

1. Jesus	• disapproved of Jesus' miracle on the Sabbath.
2. Neighbors	• was healed by Jesus and confessed Him as Lord.
3. Siloam	• asked, "How were your eyes opened?"
4. Pharisees	• said, "Who sinned, this man or his parents?"
5. Disciples	• anointed the blind man's eyes with mud.
6. The man born blind	• is the pool where the blind man washed.

Thinking about God's Word

1. What did Jesus' disciples think was the cause of the man's blindness?

2. According to Jesus, why was this man blind?

3. Describe the order of events when Jesus healed the man.

4. What reason did the Pharisees give for not believing that Jesus was sent from God?

5. How did the man describe Jesus' identity when he was questioned by the Pharisees?

6. What happened after the man was cast out?

Applying God's Word

1. In this story, Jesus reminds His disciples that He is "the light of the world." His light is needed by all people, not simply those who physically can't see. In what way are we blind without the light that Jesus brings?

2. The Pharisees accused Jesus of not keeping the Sabbath laws. Which of the Ten Commandments tells us God's law for how we should regard the day set aside for worship?

   What does this commandment mean?

3. Many people who knew the blind man were curious about how he was given sight. When they asked, the man told them all that Jesus had done for him. Jesus has done a lot for you too. Tell about His healing in your life.

89

The Good Shepherd (John 10; Psalm 23)

Reviewing God's Word

Using the words below, fill in the blanks to make each Scripture quote correct. Some words will not be used.

1. The sheep follow him, for they know his _____________.
2. The ___________ comes only to steal and kill and destroy.
3. The good shepherd lays down his _________ for the sheep.
4. I _______________ My own and My own know Me.
5. He restores my _________________.
6. Your rod and Your staff, they __________________ me.
7. Surely goodness and mercy shall ________________ me.
8. I shall dwell in the house of the LORD _______________.

faults	heart	convict	life
wolf	voice	remember	follow
comfort	hope	forever	know
protect	bless	soul	thief

Thinking about God's Word

1. Who is a thief and robber of the sheep?
2. How, specifically, does the shepherd call his sheep?
3. In John 14:6, Jesus says, "I am the way, and the truth, and the life. No one comes to the Father except through Me." Which words in this story say a very similar message?
4. What could happen if a hired hand takes care of the sheep?
5. Of whom does Jesus speak when He talks about "the sheep"?
6. Jesus compares His close relationship with His sheep (or, people) with that of His intimate connection to whom?
7. Name some of the ways that Psalm 23 describes how the Lord provides abundantly for His people.
8. Which words of Psalm 23 would be especially comforting if we or someone we know is close to death?

Applying God's Word

1. Humans have a tendency to pride themselves in being independent; that is, being able to take care of matters on their own. Sheep are not known for being smart animals and are very dependent. Why, then, would we want to be like sheep?
2. In Psalm 23, King David describes the peace he has even though the possibility of death is all around him. His comfort is that God is with him. We also have this comfort, as well as a promise sealed in a death that Jesus predicts in this story. Where is this prediction and how did this death take place? What does this mean for you?
3. Isaiah 53:7 says, "Like a lamb that is led to the slaughter, and like a sheep that before its shearers is silent, so He opened not His mouth." This verse of Scripture is not comparing us to sheep. Who is being prophesied about and what event is being described?

90

Jesus Raises Lazarus (John 11)

Reviewing God's Word

Draw a line through the sentences that are not true.

1. When Jesus learned that His friend Lazarus was ill, He rushed to go heal him.
2. Jesus first spoke to His disciples about Lazarus's death by saying that Lazarus was asleep.
3. Martha and Mary both said, "Lord, if You had been here, my brother would not have died."
4. Jesus said, "Your brother may rise again."
5. Jesus wept with Martha, Mary, and the Jews who were gathered to mourn.
6. After rolling away the stone, Jesus entered the tomb to lay His hands on Lazarus.
7. Some Jews who witnessed Lazarus's resurrection went to tell the Pharisees what He had done.

Thinking about God's Word

1. Why did the disciples misunderstand Jesus when He said Lazarus had "fallen asleep"? What did Jesus really mean?
2. Who was the first of Lazarus' sisters to greet Jesus?
3. Which of Martha's first words to Jesus show that she still had hope even during her sadness?
4. How does Mary's action upon greeting Jesus point to her trust in Him as One sent from God?
5. Because Jesus knows that His Father always hears Him, why did He pray aloud in front of Lazarus's tomb?
6. With what words did Jesus bring Lazarus back to life?
7. How did the Pharisees react when some Jews told them about Jesus raising Lazarus from the dead?

Applying God's Word

1. Why did Jesus delay in going to see Lazarus? We know He had the power to heal His friend before he died.
2. Are you ever like Martha and Mary—frustrated and confused by God's timing? Explain.
3. Jesus' power over death was certainly displayed as He resurrected the bodies of Lazarus and Jairus's daughter. But what resurrection is even more significant for us?

91

The Prodigal Son
(Luke 15)

Reviewing God's Word

Write the name of the speaker next to each quote. Some names will not be used.

1. "I am no longer worthy to be called your son."
2. "Bring quickly the best robe, and put it on him."
3. "Your brother has come."
4. "These many years I have served you."
5. "And the father divided his property between them."

servant	older son	mother
master	God	citizen
Jesus	father	younger son

Thinking about God's Word

1. What did the younger son do with his inheritance after he received it?
2. What hardship did the foreign country, in which the younger son was living, begin to experience around the time that he had spent everything?
3. Why did the son feed pigs?
4. How can you tell that the younger son was truly sorry for what he had done?
5. Find the words the son planned to use to say that he had sinned greatly and no longer deserved his father's love.
6. How can you tell that the father had been waiting for his son?

   How did the father show that he had never stopped loving his son and that he had already forgiven him?
7. What did the father mean when he said, "For this my son was dead, and is alive again"?
8. Why was the older son upset about the celebration being held for his brother?
9. Of whom is the father of this lesson a true picture?

Applying God's Word

1. Did the father approve of his son's sin? How did he show that he loved him just the same?

   How did the father's never-ending love help the son?
2. When have we acted like the younger son?

   the older son?
3. Will God ever turn away a repentant person because his or her sin is too great for forgiveness? Explain.

92

Jesus Heals Ten Men (Luke 17)

Reviewing God's Word

Fill in the blanks, using the words below. Some words will not be used.

1. Jesus traveled along the border between ______________ and Galilee.
2. __________ men with leprosy met Him.
3. They called, "Jesus, ______________, have mercy on us!"
4. Jesus told them to show themselves to the ____________.
5. One of the men came back and ______________ God in a loud voice.
6. Jesus asked, "Were not ten ______________________?"
7. Jesus said to the Samaritan, "_____________ and go your way; your __________________ has made you well."

Samaria	changed	Messiah	praised
priests	Ten	Nazareth	cleansed
Jesus	gatekeeper	younger son	faith
Master	welcomed	Five	knowledge

Thinking about God's Word

1. Where was Jesus going?

2. As Jesus entered a village, how did ten men alert Him to their need?

3. Why did the men want Jesus to have mercy on them?

4. At what point during the story did the men realize they had been cleansed?

5. Who came back to praise God?

6. What words describe how the man acted when he returned to see Jesus?

7. What did Jesus mean when He said, "Where are the nine?"

8. Why was the leper healed?

Applying God's Word

1. Tell how this account shows Jesus as the Lord and Savior of all people.

2. How have you acted like one of the nine men who did not return to give thanks to Jesus?

3. What example does the Samaritan provide for those who love and trust in Jesus as Savior? Hint: think of the ways God has restored you to health.

93

Jesus and the Little Children (Mark 9–10)

Reviewing God's Word

Underline the word or phrase that answers each question.

1. What group was discussing who was the greatest in the kingdom of heaven? (Parents—Disciples—Priests—Scribes)
2. If someone receives a child in Christ's name, whom is that person really receiving? (Disciples—Peter—Their parents—Jesus)
3. What was the disciples' reaction when people brought children to Jesus? (Rebuking—Approving—Smiling—Worrying)
4. Why did Jesus say He wanted the children to be brought to Him? (They always chased Jesus—They were calling for Him—They were orphans—The kingdom of God belonged to them)
5. What did Jesus do for the children? (Healed—Taught—Blessed—Questioned)

Thinking about God's Word

1. Why might the disciples have kept silent when Jesus asked about their discussion?

2. What must a person do to be first in God's kingdom?

3. According to Jesus, anyone who receives a child in His name is receiving Him too. If someone receives Jesus, who is that person ultimately receiving?

4. With which words did Jesus tell the disciples that they were not to keep the children away?

5. How does Jesus emphasize that all people, regardless of age, are to be like children in terms of their faith?

Applying God's Word

1. Jesus said that the greatest in His kingdom were those who were "last of all and servant of all." What does this say about people who believe they need to loudly proclaim their good works so others see what a "good" Christian they are?

2. Though God is without sin, our relationship with Him has similarities to our relationship with our earthly father. How so? In what ways does God provide beyond our fathers' capabilities?

3. What can this story tell us about the necessity to baptize babies, welcoming them into God's kingdom?

94

Jesus and Zacchaeus
(Luke 19)

Reviewing God's Word

For the following statements, circle T for true and F for false.

1. Jesus passed through Jericho.	T	F
2. A man named Zacchaeus was a chief tax collector.	T	F
3. Zacchaeus climbed into a tree so he could mock Jesus as He passed by.	T	F
4. Jesus looked up in the tree and told Zacchaeus He would be staying at his house.	T	F
5. Zacchaeus showed that he was sorry for his sins by returning four times as much as he had gotten dishonestly.	T	F
6. Jesus said, "Today salvation has passed by this man."	T	F
7. Jesus came to save what was lost.	T	F

Thinking about God's Word

1. Why did Zacchaeus decide to climb a tree when he heard Jesus was passing through?

2. How do we know that Jesus was looking for Zacchaeus when He came to the tree?

3. Why did some people grumble?

4. Was Jesus the guest of a sinner? Explain.

5. Tell how the Holy Spirit was at work in Zacchaeus's life after he was found by Jesus and received Him as his Savior.

6. Why did Jesus go with Zacchaeus?

7. In which words did Jesus give the reason for His coming into the world?

Applying God's Word

1. Isaiah 55:6 tells us to "seek the LORD while He may be found; call upon Him while He is near." This is an instruction to listen to God's Word. How did Zacchaeus, against some obstacles, respond to this? How do you?

2. How did those who grumble show that they did not understand why Jesus had come to them?

3. What does Jesus' message of salvation for Zacchaeus mean for us?

95

The Triumphal Entry (Matthew 21; Mark 11; Luke 19)

Reviewing God's Word

Underline the word or phrase that answers each question.

1. Toward which city were Jesus and His disciples going? (Capernaum—Bethlehem—Jerusalem—Jericho)

2. Which sad part of Jesus' life was soon to begin? (Hiding—Preaching—Suffering—Ascension)

3. What animals did Jesus send two disciples to find? (Donkey and colt—Horse and pony—Sheep and goat—Watch dog and tabby cat)

4. What did the disciples tell those who questioned them about taking the animals? ("Your king has come"—"It is the cause"—"The Lord needs them"—"Please, sir")

5. Who spoke the words "Say to the daughter of Zion"? (Pharisee—Moses—A prophet—The disciples)

6. What name did the multitude apply to Jesus? (Hosanna—Son of David—Rabbi—Savior)

7. If the people had not praised Jesus upon His entrance, what did He say would cry out? (Babies—Fields—Stones—Donkeys)

8. What did Jesus show Himself to be in this lesson? (Savior—Mighty—Rich—Government official)

Thinking about God's Word

1. Why did Jesus send two disciples ahead to the next village?

2. Why did Jesus want a donkey instead of another animal?

3. What were the words of the prophecy that was fulfilled?

4. Who is the daughter of Zion? Hint: what city was Jesus entering?

   Who was the king who came to the daughter of Zion?

5. How did the disciples prepare the donkey for Jesus?

6. What did the crowd do to honor Jesus as their King?

7. What did the people shout?

8. How did the Pharisees react to all of the commotion?

Applying God's Word

1. Horses were used by soldiers and kings for delivering messages and appearing before the people. Donkeys were used in the everyday life of the people. Besides fulfilling the prophecy, how did Jesus' entrance on a donkey indicate the kind of king He was?

2. The people shouted, "Hosanna to the Son of David!" *Hosanna* means "save us now." Why did they give Jesus the name "Son of David"? In what way would Jesus provide an answer to their cry during the week ahead? to your cry?

3. Jesus' entrance into Jerusalem marked the start of a very important week in His life; we call it "Holy Week." We remember this story with a celebration called "Palm Sunday." Name any other holy days you can think of that are commemorated in the days immediately following Palm Sunday.

96

The Widow's Coins (Mark 12)

Reviewing God's Word

Draw a line through the sentences that are not true.

1. Jesus was talking to a Pharisee when one of His disciples pointed to the widow.

2. The rich people at the temple put in large sums of money.

3. A widow put in one piece of silver, which was her last day's wage.

4. Jesus said, "This poor widow has put in the same amount as all those who are contributing."

5. Others who had contributed to the offering simply gave out of their abundance.

Thinking about God's Word

1. How do you think the rich people felt about their contributions?

2. Why did the widow give an offering of only two coins?

3. What do the widow's actions communicate about her faith in God?

4. What did Jesus mean when He said that the others at the temple "contributed out of their abundance"?

Applying God's Word

1. Why might Jesus have explained to His disciples His understanding of the widow's giving?

2. "The Lord sees not as man sees: man looks on the outward appearance, but the Lord looks on the heart" (1 Samuel 16:7). These words were spoken when one of Jesus' ancestors, David, was anointed as king. But this truth applies in many situations. What can this verse tell you about the widow's giving? your own?

3. What are the greatest riches you have been given?

97

The Lord's Supper (Luke 22)

Reviewing God's Word

Draw lines to match each name to the action that fits the person.

1. Judas	• sought a way to kill Jesus.
2. John	• instituted the Lord's Supper.
3. Satan	• agreed to betray Jesus in return for money.
4. Chief priests	• claimed he was ready to die with Jesus.
5. The disciples	• helped Peter prepare the Passover.
6. Peter	• entered into Judas Iscariot.
7. Jesus	• allowed Jesus to host the Passover in his home.
8. The man with a jar	• were the first recipients of the Lord's Supper.

Thinking about God's Word

1. Which great Jewish festival was drawing near at this time?

2. The chief priests took their time in devising the best way to put Jesus to death because "they feared the people." What, exactly, was their fear regarding the people?

3. From whom did Judas receive motivation to go to the chief priests?

4. What message were Peter and John supposed to tell the man with the jar of water?

5. How did Jesus tell His disciples that this would be the last Passover meal they would all share?

6. What did Jesus do with the bread before He broke it and gave it to His disciples?

   When was Jesus' body broken for us?

7. Tell what Jesus said about the bread and the cup of wine.

   With what words does Jesus indicate that this meal, His Supper, is to be received by His people in generations to come?

8. Who is the "you" that Jesus was talking about when He said His body and blood were given for "you"?

9. What did Peter tell the Lord he was ready to do with Him?

Applying God's Word

1. Exodus 12 describes God's instructions for the Passover meal. A lamb "without blemish" was sacrificed—its blood on the Israelites' doorposts sealed the safety of the people, and its flesh was eaten for their nourishment. Why was Passover a fitting time for Jesus to die for the sins of the world?

2. For what purpose did Jesus pour out His blood?

3. What else is received with the bread and wine at the Lord's supper?

   Why should God's people receive the Lord's Supper often?

98

Jesus in the Garden
(Matthew 26; Mark 14; Luke 22)

Reviewing God's Word

Circle Yes or No for each statement.

1. When Jesus and the disciples arrived at the garden, He said, "Come pray with Me."	YES	NO
2. Jesus told three disciples to keep watch with Him.	YES	NO
3. While Jesus suffered greatly, the disciples kept falling asleep.	YES	NO
4. Jesus said to them, "The spirit is not willing, and the flesh is also weak."	YES	NO
5. God sent an angel to Jesus to strengthen Him during His agony.	YES	NO
6. Judas betrayed Jesus with a common greeting of that time—a kiss.	YES	NO
7. Jesus said to Judas, "Friend, why do you come now?"	YES	NO
8. The disciples remained with Jesus as He was led away.	YES	NO

Thinking about God's Word

1. What instructions did Jesus give to all of His disciples upon arriving at Gethsemane?

   What did He specifically ask of Peter, James, and John?

2. Which words describe the change that the disciples saw coming over Jesus?

3. What did Jesus ask His Father to let pass from Him?

   What was Jesus speaking about?

4. In your own words, tell what Jesus was praying about when He said, "My Father, if it is possible, let this cup pass from Me. Nevertheless, not as I will, but as You will."

5. How does knowing that Jesus was fully man help in understanding what He was praying about?

6. What were Jesus' great drops of sweat like that fell to the ground?

7. What happened to a servant of the high priest?

8. Summarize Jesus' explanation for why swords and violence were not necessary during His arrest.

Applying God's Word

1. What example do Jesus' actions upon arriving in the garden provide for us for times when we are scared, worried, or nervous?

2. When Jesus saw Judas approaching, He said, "The Son of Man is betrayed into the hands of sinners." In what way are we, two thousand years later, part of that description?

3. How and why did the disciples react when Jesus was arrested? When might it be easy for us to act in the same way?

99

Peter Denies Jesus (Matthew 26)

Reviewing God's Word

Fill in the blanks, using the words or phrases below. Some words will not be used.

1. Peter followed Jesus to the courtyard of the ______________________________.
2. "The whole Council were seeking __________________ testimony against Jesus."
3. Jesus remained ________________ when the high priest asked Him about rebuilding the temple.
4. The high priest said Jesus spoke __________________ and therefore deserved death.
5. Two __________________ girls claimed that Peter had been with Jesus.
6. The third time Peter was confronted, he said of Jesus, "I do not ________________ the man."
7. After the rooster crowed, Peter left the courtyard to __________________.

Pilate	evil	unchanged	know
pray	like	blasphemy	high priest
good	servant	understand	remember
promises	silent	weep	false

Thinking about God's Word

1. Which words indicate that Caiaphas and the Council didn't want to give Jesus a fair trial but had already made up their minds to put Him to death?

2. It was actually not possible for Jesus to have a fair trial. Explain how this fit into God's plan for His Son.

3. Two witnesses quoted Jesus as saying that He could "destroy the temple of God" and rebuild it in three days. The people thought He was speaking literally, but what was Jesus really talking about? Hint: see page 170 of *120 Bible Stories*.

4. What was Jesus' response when the high priest asked if He was the Christ?

5. What is the meaning of the sin of blasphemy, which brought a fateful judgment on Jesus?

   Was He guilty of this sin?

6. In what part of the story do they mock Jesus' divinity?

7. What did Peter deny (not admit or confess)?

8. How is Peter's remorse over his denial clearly shown?

Applying God's Word

1. The Council determined that Jesus was deserving of death because they decided His claim to be God was blasphemous. From what you yourself have learned of Jesus' life, cite four or five actions or proclamations that indicate Jesus was the Christ.

2. In what ways did Peter disobey the commandments "You shall have no other gods" and "You shall not misuse the name of the Lord your God"?

3. How do God's people today deny Jesus as their Savior?

   Does God forgive everyone who repents of their denial? Explain.

100

Jesus' Trial (Matthew 27; John 18)

Reviewing God's Word

Underline the word or phrase that makes each sentence true.

1. Pilate was the Roman (high priest—governor—king—authority).
2. Pilate asked Jesus if He was a (God—king—Christian—Roman).
3. Jesus answered that His "(kingdom—love—leadership—Father) is not of this world."
4. "Pilate said to Jesus, "What is (hope—the way—Your purpose—truth)?"
5. Pilate told the Jews that he found in Jesus no (guilt—divinity—innocence—hope).
6. To show that he did not claim responsibility for Jesus' blood, Pilate (spit on the ground—washed his hands—summoned the guard—wept).
7. The crown that Jesus wore was made of (thorns—gold—purple—reeds).
8. When Pilate brought Jesus forth, the crowd said, ("Flog Him!"—"Here is the man!"—"Condemn Him!"—"Let Him be crucified!")

Thinking about God's Word

1. Why did Pilate ask Jesus if He was the King of the Jews?

2. The duties of a king that Pilate probably thought of—ruling a people with laws, justice, and wise decisions to keep the peace—were not the descriptions that Jesus provided of His kingship. What was Jesus' purpose in His kingdom?

3. What did Pilate mean when he told the crowd that he found no guilt in Jesus?

4. How did Pilate plan to release Jesus?

5. Explain how Pilate knew that "it was out of envy that they [the religious leaders] had delivered Jesus to him."

6. What unfair treatment did Pilate let the soldiers give Jesus, even when he knew that Jesus was without fault?

7. Did all of the Jews in Jerusalem want to see Jesus crucified?

Applying God's Word

1. In response to one of Pilate's questions, Jesus said that "everyone who is of the truth listens to My voice." How does Jesus' trial highlight the multitudes that were deaf to His voice or resisted His words?

2. The prophet Isaiah wrote of Jesus' suffering before death: "He was oppressed and He was afflicted, yet He opened not His mouth" (53:7). How were Pilate's actions part of God's plan of salvation for the world?

3. Pilate delivered Jesus to be crucified, but his decision to condemn Jesus was not why Jesus went to the cross. Who is really responsible for Jesus' death?

101

The Crucifixion (Matthew 27; Luke 23; John 19)

Reviewing God's Word

Draw a line through the sentences that are not true.

1. As the soldiers led Him to be crucified, Jesus asked God to bring revenge upon His enemies.
2. The sign that Pilate made for Jesus' cross read, "Jesus of Nazareth, the King of the Jews."
3. Jesus told one of the two criminals crucified with Him that he would enter Paradise.
4. Jesus said to His mother, "Woman, you shall see Me again."
5. From the cross, Jesus called out, "Father, into Your hands I commit My spirit."
6. The soldiers broke Jesus' legs because they were not sure if He was dead.
7. Joseph of Arimathea had never heard of Jesus, but he decided to give Him a proper burial.
8. Jesus' body was placed in a new tomb that had not yet been used.

Thinking about God's Word

1. Where was Jesus crucified?

2. What words did Pilate write on the sign that was placed above Jesus on the cross?

   Why did he choose this phrase?

3. Two criminals were crucified on either side of Jesus. The first one labeled Jesus as "the Christ," but then he taunted Him. What did he not understand about Jesus' death?

4. Which words of the other criminal show his faith in Jesus' saving work?

   What certain promise did Jesus give him?

5. What did Jesus do when He saw His mother standing at the foot of His cross?

6. What words did Jesus call out in a loud voice before He bowed His head and died?

7. One reason why Jesus' legs were not broken was because the soldiers could tell that He was already dead. Name another explanation for why His bones were not broken.

8. Toward the beginning of Jesus' ministry, Nicodemus had asked Jesus about His kingdom (see page 172 of *120 Bible Stories*). What might Nicodemus's presence at Golgotha mean?

9. Jesus had predicted His resurrection numerous times before His disciples and groups of Jewish followers. How did the actions of Joseph of Arimathea and Nicodemus show that they did not grasp this prophecy?

Applying God's Word

1. How does Jesus' prayer that God would forgive those who sentenced Him to death relate to His purpose in dying?

2. In Psalm 22:1, King David laments, "My God, my God, why have You forsaken me?" Jesus says these same words while crying out from the cross. As His children, do we need to fear being forsaken by God? Explain.

3. Jesus' death was both physically excruciating (crucifixion is a brutal process) and spiritually agonizing (He felt the weight of the world's sins and God's wrath). And yet, Hebrews 12:2 says that Jesus died "for the joy that was set before Him." What was the source of this joy?

102

The Resurrection (Luke 24; John 20)

Reviewing God's Word

For the following statements, circle T for true and F for false.

1. When the women arrived at the tomb at early dawn, the stone was not yet rolled away.	T	F
2. Two men (angels) said to the women, "Why do you seek the living among the dead?"	T	F
3. The angels reminded the women that Jesus had predicted His resurrection while He was still teaching in Galilee.	T	F
4. All the apostles rejoiced upon hearing the news of Jesus' resurrection.	T	F
5. When Jesus appeared to Mary Magdalene, she was outside the tomb by herself weeping over His absence.	T	F
6. It was not until Jesus spoke her name that Mary Magdalene recognized Jesus.	T	F
7. Jesus said to Mary Magdalene, "Do not cling to Me, for My kingdom is not of this world."	T	F
8. Jesus broke the chains of death for us.	T	F

Thinking about God's Word

1. How soon after Jesus' burial did the women travel to the tomb?

2. Were the women expecting Jesus' resurrection? Explain.

3. Why did the angels who appeared to the women mention that Jesus had already predicted His resurrection?

4. To whom did the women run to tell the news of Jesus' resurrection? What was the reaction from this group?

5. Which disciple showed by his actions that he had faith in the words of the women and this act of God?

6. Why was Mary Magdalene weeping outside the tomb?

7. Who did Mary Magdalene think Jesus was when He first appeared to her? When did she recognize Him as her Lord?

8. What did Jesus want Mary Magdalene to do rather than stay with Him?

Applying God's Word

1. In 1 Corinthians 15:14, the apostle Paul says that "if Christ has not been raised, then our preaching is in vain and your faith is in vain." What would you say to someone who claims to trust in Jesus as the Savior but does not believe in His resurrection?

2. Mary did not acknowledge the risen Jesus until He spoke to her. How does Jesus speak to people today to bring them to recognize Him as their Lord?

3. Jesus said to Mary Magdalene, "I am ascending to My Father and your Father, to My God and your God." What does this statement tell us about our relationship with God because Jesus conquered death?

103

Jesus Appears on the Emmaus Road (Luke 24)

Reviewing God's Word

Fill in the blanks, using the words below. Some words will not be used.

1. While two disciples were walking to a village called ________________, Jesus began walking alongside them.
2. Jesus said, "What are you ________________ about as you walk?"
3. Cleopas asked if Jesus was the only visitor to ________________ who was not aware of what happened.
4. The disciples said, "We had ________________ that He was the one to redeem Israel."
5. Jesus said, "O ________________ ones, and slow of heart to believe all that the ________________ have spoken!"
6. The disciples said to each other, "Did not our ____________ burn within us while He talked to us on the road?"
7. Jesus was known to them in the breaking of the ________________."

prophets	hoped	Jerusalem	Emmaus
weeping	great	bread	Bethany
promises	known	foolish	wondering
hearts	Nazareth	talking	peace

Thinking about God's Word

1. Why did the two disciples not fall down and worship Jesus when He began walking with them?
2. Why might Jesus have asked questions of which He already knew the answer?
3. According to these disciples, why was all hope lost that Jesus had come to redeem Israel?
4. List some pieces of information that the disciples shared "concerning Jesus of Nazareth."
5. What was Jesus' reaction to the disciples' profession of doubt about Jesus being the Redeemer?
6. How long did Jesus stay with these two disciples?

Applying God's Word

1. Scripture has often been described as *Christocentric*, meaning that Jesus Christ is the central importance of what was written. How could you use this story to teach that Jesus is not simply found in the New Testament?
2. The disciples recognized Jesus after He had broken bread, blessed it, and gave it to them. Of what sacrament is this reminiscent?

   How is the disciples' recognition of the Lord similar to what happens when God's people receive this sacrament in a worthy manner?
3. What immediate action did the disciples take when they realized who had just been teaching them?

   Why is it important to include the resurrection when we confess our faith to others?

104

Jesus Appears to Thomas (John 20)

Reviewing God's Word

Answer each question with a word or phrase from below. Not all words will be used.

1. On the evening of what day did Jesus appear to His disciples?
2. Whom did the disciples fear enough to stay behind locked doors?
3. Which two scarred body parts did Jesus show them?
4. Who was given to the disciples when Jesus breathed on them?
5. Which disciple wanted physical proof that Jesus was alive?
6. After how many days did Jesus reappear to the disciples?

Pilate	Two	God the Father
Thomas	Holy Spirit	Sunday
Eight	Peter	Friday
Hands and feet	Hands and side	Group of Jews

Thinking about God's Word

1. What specific words are used to describe how Jesus appeared to His disciples on both occasions?
2. With which words did Jesus greet the disciples?
3. How did the disciples react to seeing the same Jesus who had lived among them before His death?
4. What reason does Jesus give for sending out His disciples to preach?
5. What does Jesus say about the disciples' authority to not forgive someone of their sins?
6. By what words of Thomas is it clear that he instantly believed in the resurrected Lord after touching His wounds?
7. How was Jesus' disappointment in Thomas revealed?

Applying God's Word

1. Is it possible that a pastor's proclamation of forgiveness actually forgives repentant sinners in the congregation? Use Jesus' words to explain.
2. In this story, Jesus speaks about the faith that His children will have in coming generations, including yours. Which words are these?
3. How is it that a person can come to faith in Jesus as Savior if he or she has never seen the physical presence of the Lord?

105

Jesus and Peter
(John 21)

Reviewing God's Word

Circle Yes or No for each statement.

1. The disciple whom Jesus loved said, "I am going fishing."	YES	NO
2. That night, the disciples did not catch any fish.	YES	NO
3. As day was breaking, Peter saw the Lord and asked Him to come to them.	YES	NO
4. Jesus built a charcoal fire and prepared breakfast for the disciples.	YES	NO
5. Their net was not torn, despite the large number of fish they had caught.	YES	NO
6. This was the first time Jesus had appeared since His resurrection.	YES	NO
7. Jesus asked Peter to stop doubting and believe.	YES	NO

Thinking about God's Word

1. At the beginning of Jesus' ministry, He called these disciples to follow Him. List some similarities between that event and this appearance of Jesus. Hint: see page 166 of *120 Bible Stories.*

2. By what name did Jesus address the disciples at sea?

3. How did Peter react when he realized that the Lord was standing on the shore?

4. In what way did Jesus provide for the needs of the disciples after they arrived on shore?

5. Using your own words, rephrase Jesus' question to Peter, "Simon, son of John, do you love Me more than these?"

6. Why is it significant that Jesus asked Peter about his love for Him three times?

7. After Jesus inquired about Peter's love a third time, "Peter was grieved." What was probably the reason for this emotion?

Applying God's Word

1. Even after Jesus' resurrection, He continued to care for His disciples with acts of service. What are two examples in this story?

   How does Jesus serve us today?

2. Jesus gave Peter a similar instruction after every time that he confesses his love: he is to care for Jesus' sheep. Who then was Peter to tend? Hint: see page 200 of *120 Bible Stories.*

   How was he to care for them?

   Who has nurtured your spiritual growth?

3. What do you know about the source of the love that Peter confesses, according to 1 John 4:10: "In this is love, not that we have loved God but that He loved us and sent His Son to be the propitiation for our sins"?

106

Jesus Ascends to Heaven (Matthew 28; Acts 1)

Reviewing God's Word

Draw a line through the sentences that are not true. Write a corrected sentence on the blank.

1. Jesus lived on earth 40 years after His resurrection.
2. Jesus told the disciples to leave Jerusalem and start preaching immediately.
3. Before He ascended into heaven, Jesus promised to be with His disciples to the end of the age.
4. A legion of angels appeared, singing praises to God.
5. The disciples and some others returned to the upper room and devoted themselves to prayer.
6. A man named Matthias came to the upper room and asked to be a witness.

Thinking about God's Word

1. During the time that Jesus was on earth after His resurrection, what was He speaking about?
2. Before Jesus' ascension, He told His disciples that they would receive a source of power in order to be His witnesses. From where would this power come?
3. In His message to the disciples, what words of Jesus told of His divine nature?
4. List the three commands that Jesus gave to the disciples while He was still on the mountain with them.
5. In what parts of the world were the disciples to be witnesses about the Good News of Christ?
6. According to Peter, what qualifications did the new disciple need to possess?

Applying God's Word

1. All three persons of the Holy Trinity are mentioned multiple times in this story. List as many as you can find and tell what is said about each person.
2. Jesus' instructions to His disciples—to make disciples, baptize, and teach—is referred to as the Great Commission. This was the task ahead of them, but only after they had received the Holy Spirit. When did God give His Spirit to you?

   How can we fulfill the same commission given to the disciples?
3. Which words of Jesus provide a reminder that we do not need to figure out when He will come again?

   What are we to do while we wait for Him?

107

Pentecost

(Acts 2)

Reviewing God's Word

Underline the word or phrase that makes each sentence true.

1. On the day of Pentecost, the disciples were (apart—away—together—renounced).
2. (The Holy Spirit—The Son—The Father—The prophets) came upon the disciples.
3. The disciples began to speak (loudly—mournfully—different languages—in whispers).
4. Some Jews who had gathered to witness this sight thought the men were filled with (wine—wonder—good works—nonsense).
5. In response to the Jews' curiosity and doubt, (John—Luke—Peter—the disciples) gave a sermon about the truth of Christ.
6. To those in the crowd who were "cut to the heart," Peter said, "(Give up—Repent—Weep—Learn) and be baptized."
7. (Peter—The Holy Spirit—The disciples—Jews) opened the hearts of the people so that they believed in Christ and were forgiven.
8. About (30,000—300,000—3,000—300) people became Christians that day.

Thinking about God's Word

1. What signs indicated that the Holy Spirit entered the room in which the disciples were gathered?

2. By what miracle did the disciples show that the Holy Spirit had come upon them?

   Which words tell that the Holy Spirit told them what to say?

3. Other than the disciples, who witnessed the events of Pentecost?

4. Which words of the Jews who gathered give an idea of what the disciples were saying while speaking other languages?

5. Why might some of the Jews have attributed the work of the Holy Spirit to the disciples being filled with wine (drunk)?

6. Tell how Peter began the work of "catching men" that Jesus had foretold in Luke 5:9–10.

7. Why could Peter be so sure about everything that He preached about Christ?

8. How did many in the crowd respond to Peter's sermon? Why did they react this way?

Applying God's Word

1. How was the Holy's Spirit outpouring at Pentecost the fulfillment of what Jesus told His disciples at the time of His ascension? See page 236 of *120 Bible Stories*.

   Having received the Spirit, what were they prepared to do?

2. According to Peter's words to the repentant Jews, what did you receive at the time of your Baptism in addition to the Holy Spirit?

3. Are we included among the recipients of God's promise in Christ Jesus? Explain.

108

Peter and John Heal a Lame Man (Acts 3)

Reviewing God's Word

Fill in the blanks, using the words below. Some words will not be used.

1. Peter and _______________ were going up to the temple at the hour of prayer.
2. Peter said to the man, "What I do have I give to you. In the name of Jesus Christ of Nazareth, rise up and ____________________!"
3. Peter preached, "The God of our Fathers, glorified His _______________ Jesus."
4. "I know that you acted in ____________________, as did also your rulers."
5. "Turn again, that your ____________ may be blotted out."
6. "You are the sons of the prophets and of the covenant that ____________________ made."
7. "God, having raised up His servant, sent _____________ to you first, to _______________ you."

Luke	bless	ignorance	sins
servant	John	rejoice	Jesus
anoint	walk	messenger	God

Thinking about God's Word

1. Why was the lame man at the gate of the temple?

2. What did the man expect Peter and John would give him?

   Which of Peter's first words to the man might have been initially disappointing to him?

3. How did the man show his thankfulness for the healing he received?

4. According to Peter, how was this man healed?

   Why was it important for Peter to emphasize this fact to the astounded crowd?

5. In what part of Peter's message to the people did he emphasize that Jesus was written about in the Old Testament?

6. What phrase does Peter use to describe the sinfulness of all the people in his presence?

Applying God's Word

1. The lame man could not stand, due to a physical disability. Psalm 130:3 tells about an inability of all people: "If you, O Lord, should mark iniquities, O Lord, who could stand?" According to this verse, what cripples mankind? Is there a cure?

2. Peter said to the Jews, "You killed the Author of life, whom God raised from the dead." Should the blame for the death of Jesus be placed completely on that group of Jews? Explain.

3. What words of God's Law did Peter preach?

   What were Peter's words of Gospel?

   Where can you go to hear God's Law and Gospel preached?

109

God's Servant Stephen
(Acts 6–7)

Reviewing God's Word

For the following statements, circle T for true and F for false.

1. The disciples considered giving up preaching in order to care for the neglected widows. T F
2. Stephen was among the men chosen to care for the widows. T F
3. Before he was killed, Stephen was able to see a glimpse of the glory of God in heaven. T F
4. Stephen kept silent while he was being stoned. T F
5. A young man named Saul tried to save Stephen from the hands of the mob. T F

Thinking about God's Word

1. At the beginning of this story, how do the disciples' actions communicate their determination to continue sharing God's Word with the nations?

2. What did the disciples do for the appointed men before they sent them out?

3. Which words tell why Stephen could do great wonders?

4. Who stirred up the people against Stephen?

5. What accusations were brought against Stephen in front of the council?

6. Read Stephen's reply to the accusations against him. How had the fathers of the Jews been stiff-necked?

   Who was the Righteous One who had been betrayed and murdered?

7. Why is it clear that the assembly had hardened their hearts to God's Spirit?

8. Whom did Stephen see when he looked into heaven?

Applying God's Word

1. Jesus' twelve disciples were like the first pastors of the Church. According to their example, what is our pastor's duty above all else?

2. Name three specific examples of how events during the end of Stephen's life (trial and stoning) mirror similar occurrences at the end of Jesus' life on earth.

3. In 1 John 3:13, Scripture says, "Do not be surprised, brothers, that the world hates you." What does this mean for the life of Stephen?

   for you?

110

Philip and the Ethiopian

(Acts 8)

Reviewing God's Word

Fill in the blanks, using the words below. Some words will not be used.

1. Who guided Philip to find the Ethiopian? ____________
2. What was the Ethiopian doing in Jerusalem?

   ____
3. From which prophet was the man reading? __________
4. What animal was mentioned in the passage the Ethiopian was reading from in Isaiah? ____________________
5. Which person of the Trinity did Philip tell the Ethiopian about? ________________________
6. What did the Ethiopian ask for when he saw water?

   ____
7. Who removed Philip from the Ethiopian's presence?

   ____

worshiping	dove	ignorance	Isaiah
Jeremiah	Holy Spirit	drink	Jesus
help	Baptism	trading	angel
searching	walk	God	sheep

Thinking about God's Word

1. Where did the angel tell Philip to go?

2. After arriving in the desert, how did Philip know whom he should speak to?

3. What description of the man indicates his wealth and importance?

4. Why did Philip ask the man if he understood what he was reading?

5. Why was the Ethiopian confused by Isaiah's writings?

6. What evidence is there that the man's heart was not hardened to the Spirit at work in Philip's preaching of the Gospel?

7. What was the Ethiopian's attitude as he continued to travel after being baptized?

Applying God's Word

1. Explain how the prophecy the Ethiopian read was fulfilled in Jesus.

2. What about this account reminds us that salvation by grace through faith in Jesus is not only for the Israelites but also for all people?

3. How was Philip's time with the Ethiopian a fulfillment of the three parts of Jesus' Great Commission? See page 236 of *120 Bible Stories*.

111

The Conversion of Saul

(Acts 9)

Reviewing God's Word

Underline the word or phrase that answers each question.

1. Where did Saul wish to go to persecute Christians? (Samaria—Tarsus—Jerusalem—Damascus)
2. Who spoke to Saul when he fell to the ground? (The men with him—Jesus—Ananias—God the Father)
3. What happened to Saul when he got up from the ground? (He was blind—He was alone—He began to limp— He asked for Baptism)
4. What was the name of the disciple who lived at Damascus? (Peter—Ananias—Tarsus—John)
5. What did Saul do as he waited for his sight to be restored? (Cried—Prayed—Prophesied—Preached repentance)
6. When the disciple spoke to Saul, what did he call him? (Child—Poor sinner—Paul—Brother Saul)
7. Which disciple brought Saul before the others as a witness of the truth of his conversion? (Barnabas—Peter—Paul—Ananias)

Thinking about God's Word

1. How did Saul plan to persecute the Christians in the city of Damascus?
2. What is meant by the phrase "the Way"?
3. What happened to Saul on the way to Damascus?

   Whose voice was it that spoke to Saul? What did the voice say?
4. After hearing the voice, in what ways did Saul have great weakness compared to his previous days of persecuting?
5. Why did Ananias appear afraid to visit Saul?
6. With which words did Ananias assure Saul that his sins were forgiven?
7. In what three ways did Saul respond to Ananias's words?
8. After his conversion, what did Saul testify about Jesus?

Applying God's Word

1. We read in 1 Corinthians 2:14, "The natural person does not accept the things of the Spirit of God, for they are folly to him, and he is not able to understand them because they are spiritually discerned." How does this verse help explain why Saul was persecuting the Church?
2. This story points to a time when Saul received the Holy Spirit. When did this occur?

   When did God create faith in you?
3. According to Jesus, who was being persecuted when Saul harmed some of the first Christians?

   If we ever find ourselves being persecuted for our faith, what is a good way to respond? to not respond?

112

Peter and Cornelius
(Acts 10)

Reviewing God's Word

Draw a line through the sentences that are not true.

1. Cornelius was a Jew by birth, but he did not believe in God.
2. A vision of an angel with a message prompted Cornelius to send for Peter.
3. While Peter was on the housetop, he had a vision of Cornelius waiting for him.
4. Cornelius gathered many people together to hear God's Word as preached by Peter.
5. Peter did not want Cornelius to worship him.
6. As Peter spoke to the household, the Holy Spirit fell on Cornelius, not on the others in the room.
7. The Jewish believers who were with Peter disputed the Gentiles' faith.

Thinking about God's Word

1. What was Cornelius' occupation?
2. What description of Cornelius indicates that he would listen to the angel's message that came to him in a vision?
3. Retell Peter's vision from God.

   In what way did God explain the vision?
4. How did Peter know three men would be looking for him?
5. Why was Peter bothered by the fact that Cornelius fell at his feet to worship him?
6. How did Cornelius communicate that he and his household would be receptive to the message of God that Peter shared?
7. Why would it have been important for Peter to share with the group "that God shows no partiality"?
8. What did Peter command before he left?

Applying God's Word

1. According to the ceremonial law of the Old Testament, the animals that Peter saw in his vision were not to be eaten by the Jews. When God speaks, He tells Peter that this law is no longer in place. How did God use this vision to prepare Peter for visiting Cornelius?
2. Peter told Cornelius that he came to his house "without objection." Without the vision from God, why would he likely have resisted witnessing to Cornelius' household?

   Why might we object to sharing the Gospel with others who are unlike us?
3. Why were the believers who were with Peter surprised that the Holy Spirit was poured on the Gentiles?

113

Peter's Escape from Prison (Acts 12)

Reviewing God's Word

Fill in the blanks, using the words or phrases below. Some words will not be used.

King ________________ arrested some who belonged to the Church. He put Peter in __________. __________ would go on trial after the ______________. One night, an __________ appeared in Peter's cell. The __________ fell off Peter's ____________, and he was led through the city __________. Peter went to the ___________ where many fellow believers were gathered. A _____________ told the people that Peter was free.

Saul	chains	Herod	house
gate	Peter	Spirit	servant girl
neck	resurrection	angel	centurion
temple	prison	hands	Pharaoh
apostle	Passover	court	streets

Thinking about God's Word

1. Who was the first of Jesus' disciples to be killed for his faith?

   How did he die?

2. Why did King Herod arrest Peter shortly after James' death?

3. Why might Herod have decided to put four squads of soldiers in charge of guarding Peter?

4. What were members of a church doing while Peter was in prison?

5. As Peter followed the angel, did he realize that he was escaping from prison? Explain.

6. Who answered the door at the house where the church was gathered?

7. Why was the door not opened to Peter immediately?

Applying God's Word

1. What does this account reveal to us about the role of angels?

   Does God send angels to earth today?

2. Peter knew the Lord's hand had delivered him "from all that the Jewish people were expecting," meaning his death. When Jesus had been arrested, He had been condemned to die. Why did God free Peter but not His Son?

3. At the conclusion of the account, Peter tells how the Lord rescued him. How might we learn from Peter's eagerness to share about his freedom?

114

Paul's First Missionary Journey

(Acts 13–14)

Reviewing God's Word

Circle Yes or No for each statementstatement.

1. The Holy Spirit appointed work for Barnabas and Saul, and the two men set out immediately.	YES	NO
2. When Barnabas and Saul arrived at a city, they went to the synagogue.	YES	NO
3. The rulers of the synagogue in Antioch asked the men if they had any encouragement to share.	YES	NO
4. Paul's preaching did not include the fact that Jesus had died and rose to forgive the people of their sins.	YES	NO
5. The people at the synagogue begged for Paul to preach again.	YES	NO
6. Paul and Barnabas turned to preach to the Gentiles when the Good News of Jesus was rejected by the Jews.	YES	NO

Thinking about God's Word

1. In what way did the disciples prepare to send Barnabas and Saul out on their journey?

2. The Antioch synagogue rulers read from the Law and the Prophets. Why didn't they read the New Testament?

3. What was another name for Saul?

4. To whom was Paul speaking when he addressed the crowd as "men of Israel"?

5. When Paul began to preach, he did not mention the name of Jesus immediately. Whom or what did he talk about before Christ?

6. Paul used the word "promised" twice in his sermon. What promise was he talking about?

7. Why was Paul's message great news for those who still lived by the Law of Moses?

8. What reason did Paul and Barnabas give for turning to the Gentiles to preach?

Applying God's Word

1. When the angel Gabriel appeared to Jesus' mother, Mary, he said that "the Lord God will give to Him [Jesus] the throne of His father David" (page 150 of *120 Bible Stories*). Paul also highlights that Jesus is David's offspring. How does knowing Jesus' heritage help us understand God's plan of salvation?

2. Some Jews were not happy that large crowds gathered to hear this new word from God that Paul and Barnabas shared. Similarly, many Jews opposed Jesus' unfamiliar teachings. What might this tell us about how the message of the Gospel will be received by those to whom we witness?

3. On their first missionary journey, Paul and Barnabas spoke about Christ to both Jews and Gentiles. Consider how the Gospel was received by both groups. What can we learn from their witnessing experience?

115

Paul and Timothy

(Acts 16; the Books of 1 and 2 Timothy)

Reviewing God's Word

Underline the word that makes each sentence true.

1. Paul was traveling and preaching with (Barnabas—John—Silas—Peter) when he decided to have Timothy accompany them.
2. Timothy's father was a (Jew—Italian—Roman—Greek).
3. Paul called Timothy his "true (servant—child—brother—father) in the faith."
4. Paul wrote to Timothy that Jesus displays "His perfect (patience—resistance—hope—guidance) as an example of those who were to believe in Him for eternal life."
5. "For God gave us a spirit not of (forgiveness—restlessness—fear—confusion) but of power and love and (peace—mystery—self-control—hatred)."
6. "I have finished the race, I have kept the (faith—promise—Law—joy)."

Thinking about God's Word

1. Why did Paul want Timothy to accompany him and Silas on their missionary journey?
2. Which words indicate that the Holy Spirit was at work in the early Church, opening hearts to receive the Good News?
3. Whom did Jesus come into the world to save?

   Which people are these?
4. Why did Paul call himself "the foremost" of sinners? See page 248 of *120 Bible Stories.*
5. What words did Paul use to describe the Christian faith as a battle?
6. In what ways did Paul encourage Timothy to not abandon his confession of the faith and the preaching of the Word?
7. How did Paul reference that Timothy's faith had been given to him as a child?
8. With what phrase (in the last paragraph) did Paul describe eternal life in heaven?

Applying God's Word

1. In Paul's letters to Timothy, he speaks of his position in the Church. How does he describe his authority as an apostle?

   In what way do these words also apply to our pastors?
2. Paul told Timothy to "fight the good fight of the faith." In what way is being a Christian like being at war?
3. Paul said that all the faithful in Christ will receive "the crown of righteousness" on "that Day." What day is that? With what attitude may Christians anticipate this day?

116

Paul Tells Lydia about Christ; Paul Writes to the Philippians (Acts 16; Philippians 1; 4)

Reviewing God's Word

For the following statements, circle T for true and F for false.

1. One night, Jesus appeared at Paul's side and urged him to go to Macedonia.	T	F
2. Paul sailed to Troas, a leading city of the district of Macedonia.	T	F
3. Some women were gathered near the riverside where Paul went to pray.	T	F
4. After Lydia was baptized, she volunteered to sew clothes for Paul's journey.	T	F
5. He who began a good work in you will bring it to completion.	T	F
6. Let your problems be known to everyone.	T	F
7. Do not be anxious about some things.	T	F
8. God's peace will guard your hearts and your minds in Christ Jesus.	T	F

Thinking about God's Word

1. Luke wrote the Book of Acts. How is his presence with Paul recorded in this account?

2. Even before he left for Macedonia, Paul knew the purpose for which he had been sent. What was this purpose?

3. How did Paul and Luke plan to honor the Sabbath day?

Why did their plans partially change once they arrived at the riverside?

4. What was Lydia's occupation?

5. Why was Lydia able to come to faith in Jesus?

6. In what words did Paul tell the Philippians that he had not forgotten about them despite his physical separation from them?

7. When is "the day of Jesus Christ"?

8. According to Paul, what type of comfort are Christians given after they take their concerns to God in prayer?

Applying God's Word

1. When Paul and Luke went to the riverside to pray, they were not likely expecting to witness to a group of women that day. But God had other plans. What can we learn from this?

2. Paul told Timothy to "rejoice in the Lord always." How is it possible for us to rejoice even when bad situations happen in our lives?

3. Paul says that instead of being anxious, we should let our "requests be made known to God" in prayer. What specific worries might you pray about rather than allowing them to trouble your heart and mind?

117

Paul and Silas in Prison
(Acts 16)

Reviewing God's Word

Draw a line through the sentences that are not true.

1. Paul hired a slave girl to tell others about him and Silas, but he soon became annoyed with her.
2. After being accused of speaking about unlawful customs, Paul and Silas were beat with rods.
3. Paul and Silas sat in the inner prison, silently praying that they would be released.
4. A great earthquake loosed the bonds of all the prisoners.
5. The jailer nearly killed himself because he thought the prisoners had escaped.
6. As soon as they were free, Paul and Silas ran to tell the good news to other believers.
7. Paul and Silas shared the Gospel with the jailer and the members of his household.

Thinking about God's Word

1. What was the slave girl saying about Paul and Silas as she followed them?
2. Why were the girl's owners angry with Paul and Silas?
3. List some ways in which Paul and Silas were verbally and physically afflicted because of their confession of Christ.
4. How did Paul and Silas spend their time in prison?
5. Which words of Paul did God use to save the jailer's physical life?

   his soul?
6. In what way did the jailer provide for Paul and Silas's physical needs after they told him and his family about salvation in Jesus?
7. The jailer and his family was not the only group that Paul and Silas witnessed to during their night in prison. Who else may have come to faith at that time?

Applying God's Word

1. How does the unjust treatment of Paul and Silas reflect that of Jesus, beginning from when He was arrested and brought before the high priest?
2. Fellow prisoners with Paul and Silas may have come to saving faith that night. What can this part of the story tell about how the Holy Spirit works through our actions to guide others to the truth about Christ?
3. The jailer asked, "What must I do to be saved?" In what way does this question point to a common belief that humans hold regarding their salvation?

118

Paul's Letters
(The Books of Romans; Ephesians; 1 Thessalonians)

Reviewing God's Word

Fill in the blanks, using the words below. Some words will not be used.

1. "For I am not ____________ of the Gospel."
2. "The righteous shall live by ____________."
3. "God . . . even when we were ____________ in our trespasses, made us alive together with ____________."
4. "For we are His ____________, created in Christ Jesus for good ____________."
5. "When you received the Word of God, which you heard from us, you ____________ it not as the word of men."
6. "May the Lord establish your hearts ____________ in holiness before our God and Father."

lives	pride	accepted
faith	workmanship	dead
works	understanding	partial
rejected	Christ	truth
Moses	blameless	ashamed

Thinking about God's Word

1. Describe Paul's attitude toward preaching the Gospel to the Romans.
2. Why did Paul see a need to tell the Romans that salvation belonged "also to the Greek"?
3. What did Paul say the Romans would experience because they have been justified by faith?
4. In his Letter to the Ephesians, what phrase did Paul use to describe the meaning of "saint"?
5. Why did Paul make a point of telling the Ephesians that their salvation was not their "own doing"?
6. Which of Paul's words in his Letter to the Ephesians tell that God knows every detail of our future and plans it to happen in an exact way?
7. For what reason was Paul thankful for the Thessalonians?
8. According to Paul's First Letter to the Thessalonians, what would be a mistake when receiving the Word of God?

Applying God's Word

1. When Paul greeted the Ephesians, he called them saints because they "are faithful in Christ Jesus." Are we, sinners who fall short of God's Law, saints as well? Explain.
2. Some people say that in order for Jesus to save you, you must make a decision to follow Him. If "we were dead in our trespasses" when God gave us new life, is it really possible that we could decide we need a Savior? Explain.
3. Is the Bible only a collection of stories and ideas that men wrote down about God? Share your answer using Paul's argument.

119

Paul Sails to Rome
(Acts 27–28)

Reviewing God's Word

Underline the word that makes each sentence true.

1. Paul was sailing to (Rome—Antioch—Malta—Philippi).
2. Julius allowed Paul to receive the care of (warmth—medicine—friends—God) while on the journey.
3. A (cry—storm—famine—fight) came up while the group was at sea.
4. The sailors began to throw (Paul—Paul's friends—cargo—themselves) overboard.
5. Paul said, "I urge you to take heart, for there will be no loss of (morale—food—sight—life) among you."
6. On the island of Malta, the native people showed the shipwrecked group unusual (hostility—kindness—wealth—curiosity).
7. When Paul finally arrived in Rome, the (women—Roman officials—brothers—high priest) came to meet him and his friends.

Thinking about God's Word

1. Why was Paul sailing to Rome?
2. Who was Julius?
3. Paul had spent much time at sea when he made the observation that their journey would be dangerous. But, to whom did Julius listen instead of Paul?
4. Which words indicate that the storm did not last for only a matter of hours?
5. What encouragement did Paul offer the hungry men?
6. What did the soldiers plan to do when the ship hit land? Why?
7. How did Julius take action to save Paul and those with him?

Applying God's Word

1. Paul told the sailors that God would save them. To what message of greater salvation had Paul dedicated his life?
2. Once Paul arrived in Rome and was met by the brothers, his first response was to thank God. What might we learn from Paul's example?
3. Tell how this account from Paul's journey is a metaphor of the Christian life.

120

John's Vision of Heaven (Revelation 21–22)

Reviewing God's Word

Circle Yes or No for each statement.

1. The dwelling place of God is not with man. Instead, He will dwell above them.	YES	NO
2. In this new Jerusalem, death shall be no more.	YES	NO
3. The gates of the city will bear inscriptions of the sermons of Jesus and Paul.	YES	NO
4. A temple made of gold will be shining in the center of the city.	YES	NO
5. Rather than a sun or moon, the city is lit by the glory of God.	YES	NO
6. The tree of life was on either side of the flowing river.	YES	NO
7. Both the Spirit and the Bridegroom say, "Come."	YES	NO

Thinking about God's Word

1. What is the name of the holy city?

   How will this city be prepared?

2. The loud voice that John heard told him what would not be a part of life in this city. Name some of these things.

3. In what two ways does John state that the water of life will not cost anything to God's people?

4. What will be on the twelve foundations of the city's wall?

5. Who is "the Lamb"? Hint: see John the Baptist's words on page 166 of *120 Bible Stories*.

6. Why is there no need for a temple in this coming holy city?

7. By the city's light, or the glory of God, "will the nations walk." What is meant by "the nations"?

8. What did Jesus reveal to John regarding the time when He would be returning?

Applying God's Word

1. Revelation describes the new Jerusalem as the Bride of Christ. A husband is to love and provide for his wife, as well as protect her and make sacrifices for her. With these things in mind, how is Christ a perfect Husband to the Church?

2. Jesus said He will freely give "the water of life" to anyone who is thirsty. What life-giving water does God give to us right now? How does this water prepare us for the holy city?

3. Genesis 2:9 says that "the tree of life was in the midst of the garden" when God created the world. The tree of life will also be in the new Jerusalem. What happened in the Garden of Eden that will not be part of the new Jerusalem? (See page 10 of *120 Bible Stories*.) Why is this a reason to rejoice?